From the

Heart

of a

Parent

Al Millergren, Ph.D. with Paul Evans

ISBN   0-9663339-2-6

Evans, Paul
Millergren, AL

From the Heart of a Parent

Al dedicates this book to:

Connie, my wife of thirty wonderful years
and to my son Lee and my daughter Joy.

Paul dedicates this book to:

My wife Marla, and our two boys,
Sam and Steven.

From the Heart of a Parent
600 Practical Parenting Insights For Christian Parents Of Adolescents
Table of Contents

INTRODUCTION:

*H*ave you ever heard someone say, "my child will never do that," or "my child will never be allowed to act that way"? If I have ever said that, and I probably have, I can assure you that it was before I had children of my own. I positively assure you that it was before my children reached the adolescent years. Mark Twain might have had a great idea when he stated, "When your child turns twelve you should put him in a barrel, nail the lid down and feed him through a knothole. When he turns sixteen, plug the hole." If you have an adolescent in your home you probably have had very similar feelings on occasion.

We as parents seem to sail through those great pre-teen years with a lot of confidence and ease. Very few problems arise which we can't handle. All of a sudden our child reaches twelve or thirteen and things begin a dramatic change. They are now in junior high and someone or some school activity seems to be their focus. Someone other than parents begin to make a strong impact on their lives. Whether they have an eye on a person of the opposite sex or a new set of friends, the change begins. Many parents sail through this period with little effort, but many face a tumultuous few years.

The book you are holding in your hand will supply you with *600 practical insights plus 60 letters of encouragement* from parents and teens who have been there. It is my prayer that "From the Heart of a Parent" will help you and your adolescent through those years of uncertainty. Uncertainty because your teen has never been a teen before and you have never been the parent of this particular teen before.

This book idea came about when my wife wrote a letter to our son at a challenging period during his adolescence. It is printed after this introduction so you will know this book is from someone who has been where you are, or where you are headed.

There are three keys to receiving the greatest blessing from each chapter. *Prayer, consistency, and being the right role model.* The combination of the three when applied with the tips that fit your situation will enhance your parenting.

I want to encourage you to hang in there. There is a light at the end of the tunnel. Rick Muchow sings, "Don't give up, someone really loves you. Don't give up, someone really cares. Don't give up, someone really loves you and that someone is the Lord."

Keep the faith,
Al

Dear Son,

Is there any such thing as loving someone too much? If there is, I may be guilty. If loving you too much means losing my cool because of the fear of you messing up your future,
    I'm guilty!

If it's putting our relationship in jeopardy because I can't bury my head in the sand and ignore what I know,
    I'm guilty!

If loving you too much means being more headstrong and stubborn than you to protect you,
    I'm guilty!

If it is not allowing you to be selfish and inconsiderate to other people because I know it will make you an unhappy person,
    I'm guilty!

If loving you too much means not allowing you to react in a negative way during a ballgame because of the influence it has on others, which is important to your salvation,
    I'm guilty!

If it's not giving you everything you want because I see it not making you the best you can be,
    I'm guilty!

If it is nagging and repeating myself and ranting and raving

because I'm afraid of not getting through to you - yes,
I'm guilty!

If loving a person too much is forcing them to be responsible
for their own behavior because learning that at a young age
will save many heartaches,
I'm guilty!

If it is doing what breaks my heart and hurts me so badly I
want to die because it is best for you,
I'm guilty!

If loving you too much means making you mad at me for
taking away certain music or television shows because I
can't stand to let the wrong things go into your brain,
I'm guilty!

If it means putting my own happiness and peace on hold for
a few years because I won't do things the easy way and
pretend it's all fine to keep from dealing with what Satan is
trying to do to you,
I'm guilty!

If loving someone too much means requiring them to make
certain grades on their report card because it will affect
their future,
I'm guilty!

I'm guilty of demanding you prepare for your future because
I know that the next few years are the most important years
of your life since they will determine your happiness for the
rest of your life.

There are things you must do now to make the rest of
your life good. And there are things you must do now to
assure an easier and happier future.
I am guilty of wanting you to prepare and insisting that
you not blow it - even at the expense of my own peace and
happiness.
But most of all...If loving someone too much means
doing whatever it takes to get them to heaven,

I'm guilty!

There is one thing I want to have taught you, if nothing else and that is that no man is an island unto himself. Everything you do and say will affect the people around you, especially the ones you love. It can hurt them or it can help them, but it will do one or the other. Please don't ever believe that you can do as you please and it won't matter because it's your life and you own it. That is a lie and it always has been and always will be. Learn to think about how what you do has consequences; consequences that affect many people and not just yourself.

The truth is that happiness comes from thinking of others and getting out of yourself because if you don't, you will become miserable trying to make yourself happy. I don't know why this is the way it is, except I guess that's the way God made us.

A mother's love is the deepest and strongest love known to mankind, and I'm guilty of having a double dose of it for you. My greatest desire in life is to see you happy now and go to heaven later. I live to see that. I'd give up everything I own, including my life, to see that happen. It is what my very existence is about. Even in our worst moments, please know that everything I do is motivated by my love for you. When God gave you to me I promised Him I would do everything in my power to give you back to Him. I have never wavered from that goal. I know everything is going to be all right with you because I pray for you every single day at least a dozen times and I know that my Father in heaven will not let me down. He will take up the slack when I fail because I am only human and I make too many mistakes.

I wanted to write this letter because I am afraid I have gotten things to the point of you not wanting to listen anymore. I don't blame you for that and I will try to do better. Please forgive me for all the times I have lost my temper and said things that were unnecessary. My temper has been what the devil uses to get me, and I have to work very hard to control it. But, like anything else, I control it if

I want to. God promised we will never be tempted beyond what we can withstand. He will not let the devil go that far. So it is up to us to see that we do our part.

I am so thankful for you and have been every day of your life. When I thought I would never have any children, I wondered what the Lord had in mind. Now I understand that what I had in mind for me was not what was best for me. You were what is best for me and I am so thankful to God that I was never able to have children. It turned out to be the best thing that has ever happened to me!

I LOVE YOU!

Mama
(Connie Millergren)

Chapter 1

10 Reasons We Need Strong Parents

1. Develop In Your Teen A Personal Faith In God.

Ecclesiastes 9:10 says, "Whatever your hand finds to do, do it with all of your might..." Certainly raising our children and developing spiritual relationships is the ultimate "whatever."

Parenthood is one of the most pressure-packed vocations a person can experience, so "all your might" is not an option, but a requirement. Tie each moment to God and not to a phrase like, "Because I said so." Explain and model the spiritual significance of your decisions.

2. Families Are Collapsing.

Families are falling apart at a rapid rate. Children are being neglected because of parents' jobs, abuse, and divorce. Many families no longer communicate as in previous decades because of media, music, and microwaves, just to name a few.

How firm is your household's foundation? Is there serious rotting among your relationships? Study the structure of your family. How much time do you share together? When was the last meal that brought the entire crew to the table? Set aside a minimum of one night per week to eat and discuss your relationships.

3. Teen Sexuality.

Teens seem to no longer be afraid of diseases or pregnancy. Many girls give their bodies to the nearest "I love you." Guys forfeit their virginity to prove their manhood, and all of this is wrapped in the heated hormones of adolescence.

Teach teens the reason behind God's rules of purity. Read Ephesians 5:3 & I Corinthians 6:19-20 together and talk about God's desires compared to the heart's desires.

4. Teen Substance Abuse Is On The Incline.

The University of Michigan's Institute for Social Research reports that 54.3 percent of students had used an illicit drug by the time they reached their senior year of high school. Each year more and more teens become alcoholics, and nicotine & drug addicts. They use these substances to escape life, to end life, or to live up to the expectations of their peers.

Inform yourself about substance risks, then inform your teen without accusing him or her. Log on to http://www.nida.nih.gov/NIDAHome2.html for information and statistics about teens and drugs.

5. Unhealthy Media Overload.

We are parenting the first wireless generation as proven by the comic strip "Zits." Jeremy emails his mom from upstairs to ask what's for dinner? No one has to meet face-to-face, or even voice-to-voice. Email and chat rooms replace personal interaction most of the time.

First, talk and listen. Even if it's just to ask, "How was your day?" Second, regulate the media influences by getting unplugged. Set aside specific periods each week where the television, radio, computer will be unplugged and use that time to share your lives. Never allow people or events to come into your home via media that you would not have in person.

Also, consider blocks on your computer to keep certain sites out of your home.

6. Morality Is On The Decline.

If sitcoms and teen nighttime soap operas reflect the values of today's young person, we can assume that premarital sexual activity, binge drinking, and hurting others to get ahead have become the new standards.

Create on paper a set of core values for your family. What areas as a family, not just for your teen, will you refuse to compromise? What standards will become nonnegotiable?

7. Peer Pressure Will Always Be An Issue.

Acceptance and love remains the number one longing of

today's young person. The need to fit in can be so over-whelming that teenagers will lower their virtues in order to match a certain peer group.

Guide your teen toward God-esteem instead of self-esteem. Explore Romans 5:6-8 with your child.

8. Teen Violence Is Increasing.

The massacres at Columbine High School and other in-stitutions uncovered the eyes of society in relation to teen brutality. Even more shocking is the recent incident involv-ing the rape of a four-year-old girl by an eight-year-old boy.

Increase your awareness of your children's activities without prying. Do you know the names of their friends? Do you know where they spend their time? Are you aware of the influences that touch their lives? Do you know where they are going via the Internet?

9. To Provide A Safe Haven.

Teenagers are prone to adopt an "everyone is against me" attitude. Their friends tend to gossip. Dating relation-ships dissolve. Cheerleading and sports don't always deliver the popularity they promise. Home needs to be a place where teens know they won't be judged wrongfully, or be ex-pected to live up to some unattainable expectation.

10. Society's Spiritual Exploration.

That sounds positive, doesn't it? The danger is that our culture is exploring every form of spirituality from crystals to angel worship. Spirituality is on the rise, but Christianity is not the fastest growing spiritual group.

Stress relationship over ritual. Many methods of spiritu-ality focus on freedom rather than faith. The Father desires followers who trust in Him, not those seeking fulfillment through their own power (Read Hebrews 11).

Dear Parents,

We witness more and more problems with teens growing up in America today. We are shocked by the decline in morals, the rampant use of drugs, and the unbridled outpouring of violence. We would all agree that something has gone terribly wrong in our culture. However, it is too easy for us as Christians to simply point a condemning finger at our culture and not take responsibility for what we can do to make a difference in our teens. That's what this book is all about, giving us the tools to be good parents. As I have heard Al Millergren say hundreds of times, "the bottom line is getting our teens to heaven." What could be more important? Surely, that will be a better barometer of the success or failure of our lives than the size of our bank account, the productivity of our portfolio, or the worth of our possessions. Let's put our greatest effort in the eternal--our teens. Jesus would say that is "laying up treasure in heaven." Let's do more than just bemoan what is happening in our culture, let's raise Godly teens who will make a difference on this earth and spend eternity in heaven!

We believe as parents that we should listen to the words of Paul as he instructed Timothy in I Timothy 4:12-16. "Don't let anyone look down on you because you are young, but set an example for the believers in speech, in life, in love, in faith and in purity. Until I come, devote yourself to the public reading of Scripture, to preaching and to teaching. Do not neglect your gift, which was given you through a prophetic message when the body of elders laid their hands on you. Be diligent in these matters; give yourself wholly to them, so that everyone may see your progress. Watch your life and doctrine closely. Persevere in them, because if you do, you will save both yourself and your hearers." It will take strong parenting if we are going to accomplish the teachings in this passage. Ask God for wisdom and direction as you try as hard as you can to accomplish your God-given responsibility of getting your teen to heaven.

Serving Him,
Buddy and Stephanie Bell

Chapter 2

10 Tips For Daily Parenting

1. Share a Blessing.

Talk of blessings like Jesus, food, shelter, clothing, etc. It is these sweet, simple things in life that allow us to see a blessing wherever we go. Drawing attention to God's blessings plants the seed of thanksgiving in the hearts of your teens. As they mature, it will produce fruit into the lives of your grandchildren.

2. Speak Positively.

Teens live in a world of cut downs and cut ups. Their esteem is battered by words like, "Dork," "Dweeb," and "Geek." No wonder they come home in a bad mood.

Use words and phrases that build up rather than tear down. Say, "I am proud of the 'B' you made on your report," rather than, "A 'B'? If you had studied harder you could have made an 'A+'."

3. Give Hugs.

Never underestimate the power of a reassuring touch. A hug allows you to say "I love you" without using words. In a recent youth group survey, young people stated that hugs were especially critical during challenging periods of life.

Engage various hugs according to the situation. Use a playful hug after an achievement. Use a tender hug after a break-up.

4. Be A Joy-filled Parent.

Have you ever seen a person who looked like he had been dipped in vinegar while sucking a lemon? Being filled with joy doesn't mean you can't have cranky moments. It does mean that your children will see how the blessings you share impact your life.

Separate joy from happiness. Happiness is determined

by your circumstances, while joy remains regardless of the situation. Unhappiness is caused by accidents, hateful words, etc. Joy continues when our car is dented, but our souls are not.

5. Write Meaningful Notes.

This sounds "corny," doesn't it? Write my teen a note? They would laugh me out of the house. Don't kid yourself. Whether they admit it or not, most teens love to get a note as long as it doesn't show up in their lunch bag while surrounded by friends.

Use sticky notes. Stick one on the morning juice glass, "Hope you have a bright day." Slap one on the bathroom mirror, "Every time I look at you I see God's love."

6. Instill Spiritual Habits.

As a child, I remember seeing an open Bible across the table from me each morning at breakfast. I knew my mom had been reading and praying long before my eyes opened to the day.

Make prayer, Bible study, Scripture memorization, and meditation a daily practice in your home. Read Deuteronomy 6:4-8 for God's original plan.

7. Show Affection To Your Spouse.

Nothing can get a good "yuck" or "gross" out of your teen like giving your mate a kiss. Your kids can't imagine that you would ever be physically intimate.

Openly display your affection for your spouse without putting on a risqué show. Holding hands, kissing, and hugging will provide a positive picture of marriage to your teen, and help him or her know that you constantly work on your partnership.

8. Respect Your Teen's Privacy.

Privacy is an earned privilege. The more responsibility and trustworthiness a teen exhibits, the greater amount of pure privacy they deserve.

Let your teen know that you understand the need for privacy. Explain, as well, that unmonitored phone, Internet, and media privileges will not be the "norm" in the household.

9. Be Kind To Your Teen's Friends.

Most parents can find a way to embarrass their children without even trying. Failing to treat a young guest with respect and care takes embarrassment to a new level and constructs a wall between you and your teen.

Never make derogatory comments about his or her friends' clothing, hairstyle, or the way they walk and express themselves. If you sense that their cosmetics are tied to character, then discuss it with your child without placing judgment.

10. Be A Daily Learner.

Parents around the globe agree that a know-it-all attitude in their teens frustrates them. We forget, however, that teens don't like a know-it-all attitude in their parents either.

Express openly in your family your desire to grow as a parent. Read books and try new approaches to parenting. Help your teen see your wisdom by nurturing a learner's attitude that proves you haven't "arrived."

Dear Parents,

I must tell you I have re-written this letter many times. Almost daily my thoughts have changed. Just as I would make a profound statement or share some bit of advice, something would happen in our family that would make it almost laughable. That is how it goes with daily parenting. You just never know what the day may hold. The wonderful news is that we do know who holds the day. Praise God for His unchanging hand. He has spoken to my heart and made me to realize that I must freely and on a daily basis turn my children over to Him. Every day as a parent must be spent in constant prayer. We must daily lay our children at the foot of the cross. Our goal is to use each day to God's glory and prepare our children for His glorious return. Without God as the focus of our day-to-day parenting we only prepare for tomorrow-with God as our focus we prepare for eternity with Him. God says it best through Moses in

Deuteronomy 6:4-9.

Hear, O Israel: The Lord our God, the Lord is one. Love the Lord your God with all your heart and with all your soul and with all your strength. These commandments that I give you today are to be upon your hearts. Impress them on your children. Talk about them when you sit at home and when you walk along the road, when you lie down and when you get up. Tie them as symbols on your hands and bind them on your foreheads. Write them on the doorframes of your houses and on your gates.

God depends on us daily to direct our children toward Him. May we, like Hannah, vow to give our children daily to the Lord for all the days of their lives.

> In His Service,
> Mark & Julie Courson

Chapter 3

10 "Be's" For Successful Parenting

1. Be Prayerful.

James 5:16 says, "...The prayer of a righteous man is powerful and effective." Prayer causes things to happen that will not occur if we do not ask. The thought of God granting our requests should make us wear our knees out for our children.

Keep a schedule of your teen's day with you at all times. Use work breaks, sitting in the drive-through, and red lights to pray specifically for your teen concerning the activity at that time of day.

2. Be A Positive Example.

Can we say as Paul did, "Follow my example as I follow the example of Christ"? From the time of our children's birth, our lives are their Bibles, and our influence their spiritual guide.

Do you remember the childhood song *O Be Careful Little Eyes*? Use those lyrics to remind yourself that your teen watches everything you do. Measure your teaching against your life. For example, it would be impossible to convince your teen not to smoke if you are holding a cigarette while explaining the dangers of smoking.

3. Be Consistent.

Jesus warned His followers about the Pharisees, "Do as they say, but not as they do, for they say and do not." He went on to call them hypocrites. Our teens will call us the same thing if our lives and words fail to match.

Our children do notice when we tell them to say we're not home if we get an unwanted call. They pick up on our inconsistency and desire to see in us the same level of holiness that we require of them.

4. Be A Disciplinarian.

Distinguish between discipline and punishment. Discipline means you are attempting to shape character, while punishment implies payback.

When there is an unwanted attitude or action displayed, explain the discipline you are using and the appropriate behavior that should result.

5. Be Firm.

Never get into a power struggle with your child. If teens notice that their parents will give in with a little persistence, they will never stop using it to their advantage. Every young person believes they know how to pull the right strings and manipulate their parents. Make it clear that you are the authority of the home. Let your "yes" be "yes" and your "no" be "no."

6. Be Encouraging.

When Jesus came up from the water at His baptism, a voice from heaven said, "This is my beloved Son, listen to Him." Today's translation might read, "That's my Boy. I'm proud of Him."

Praise and encourage your teens so they will know they are needed and wanted. They don't want to feel like you can't wait for them to grow up and get out on their own. Catch your teens doing something right. Point out their successes and pour on the praise.

7. Be Problem-Centered.

When chaos fills your home, focus on the problem, not the person. Our natural tendency is to direct our anger and comments toward an individual, rather than an action. Jesus is the ultimate example as He loves the sinner, but hates the sin.

Consider the direction of your comments. It really does make a difference to say, "That was a foolish decision," instead of "You're an idiot!" When families recognize the separation of problem and person, each member will begin to take more responsibility for his or her actions.

24

8. Be Adventurous.

Most of us as parents want to set the safest, most protective path for our teens. Safeguarding our children is a worthy attribute, but allowing them to take some healthy risks is acceptable as well. Provide some room for failure so they can mature in all areas of life, not just the safe areas.

After a fall it's nice to have someone to pull you up and help dust you off. We need to be there for our teens when they fall by holding out a supporting hand for them to grab and get back on their feet.

9. Be Clear.

Lack of communication skills is one of the major problems families encounter today. There are three main areas of miscommunication: 1) Tone. Our emotions flow through our volume and pitch. We may be trying to explain how much we love our family, but we come across like we hate them. 2) Failure to listen. Most of us do more talking than listening, so we only get to hear our side of the story. 3) Assumption. Have you ever felt that you were clearly communicating, only to discover later that no one knew what you were talking about? Study and practice chapters 9 and 10 in this book.

10. Be Loving.

God is love (I John 4:4). Love is not what He does, but what He is. Love is what He desires for us to be as well. As God displayed His unconditional love for us, let's show our unconditional love for our families. Sure, they often get on our nerves and we don't think we can survive these trying years, but with love we will.

Read I Corinthians 13:4-8 three times. First, read it as it is written. The second time, replace the word love with God. Third time through, replace the word love with your name. Can we honestly say that is a description of us?

Dear Parents,

To be or not to be, that is the question! I would like to encourage you to be all that you can be. As I type this letter my husband and son are on their way to get my son settled in for his second year of college. While we have one teen who's living away, we have two teens still at home so we're patiently awaiting the outcome of our parenting.

I find it hard to be objective while in the middle of a process, so when we were asked to write a letter to encourage parents what "to be," I felt inept. That's when I decided to ask the kids what they thought was important for parents "to be?" Following is their input. The eldest said "Be there." He talked about how he appreciated us for being available to listen and do things together. He said he felt it was important for parents to have both quality and quantity time with their teens. It encouraged him for us to take time out for him even though it might be a sacrifice.

Our oldest daughter said, "Be supportive." She spoke about how important it was to her that we supported her in her relationships, whether it be with Christ, family, other Christians and friends, or teammates. She talked about how encouraging it was to her for us to be supportive in any extra-curricular activities she was involved in.

Our youngest daughter said, "Be consistent." She expressed how important it was to her for us to mean what we say and to stand by it. She thought it was good when kids have to learn by natural consequences from their misbehavior. She felt it was important also to be consistent with discipline. This was what, at times, kept her from making poor choices.

With our teens having had their say, all that's left is for David and me to have ours. David felt he would encourage parents to "Be a good listener." Listen to your teens and let them have some input into decisions for the family. Listen and let them talk rather than parents doing all the telling.

I guess I have two "be's" for parents. First I would say to "Be prayerful." No one knows your teen better or loves them more than God, so take everything concerning your teen to Him and trust Him. Pray for guidance. Pray for wisdom. You can pray for humility, but that usually comes with being a parent. Pray for acceptance of His will for your life.

And finally, I would like to encourage parents to "Be

real." Don't tell your teens how they need to live, show them. When you mess up or make a mistake, let your teens see you pick yourself up and start again. When you wrong someone in the family, ask them for forgiveness. Let your teens know you have weaknesses. Ask them to pray for you. Let your teens see you not want to do something, but do it anyway because it is the right thing to do. Above all, let your teens know how much you love them. Tell them and show them.

In Christian Love,
David and Susan Clark

Chapter 4

10 Tips For Creating Positive Teens

1. Display Your Own Positive Side.

The first step in helping your teen to become more positive is to take a self-evaluation. Think about recent conversations and actions. If you were your teen, would you consider yourself a positive person? Do you point out the positive more than the negative? Do you see the good inside others, or do you think the worst until it is proven otherwise?

Read Philippians 4:8-9. List the qualities on a sheet of paper that Paul encourages us to think about. Use those attitudes as a filter for the way you speak and react.

2. Set Positive Expectations.

Negatives from every angle bombard teens. No wonder they seem sour sometimes. We expect our children to clean their rooms and take out the trash, why not expect them to be positive? When they arrive home from school, work, or play set a general rule that commits them to share something positive before something negative, and you do the same.

3. Exhibit Positive Praise.

Someone suggested the best way to get rid of a minister is to pat him on the back. He will work himself to death to keep receiving the accolades. Think about it. Don't we respond to praise better than criticism? Praise works the same for our teens as it does for us.

Give praise in the form of two "L's": liberally and lavishly. Flood your child's spirit with the good things you see in him or her. Be excessive with praise, and stingy with faults.

4. Instill Positive Success.

Let's face it, every teen cannot be the captain of the football team, carry a 4.0 grade point average, and have a string of peers demanding a date. Unfortunately, many teens feel that they have to live up to those expectations.

Define "success" for your family. Let your teens know that a high grade point is wonderful, but determining their God-granted purpose is more critical. Let them know you care about sports if they do, but you care more about their souls.

5. Use God's Gifts Positively.

Once you have defined success with your teen, next help him or her discover a talent to use for God's glory. Various studies have shown that individuals who participate in the arts excel in other areas of their lives as well, which quickly aids a positive attitude.

Encourage but do not force your child to follow a talent or giftedness in an area. If he or she does not want to expand a talent at this point, pressing the issues will not alleviate family tension.

6. Explain The "Positives" Of Failure.

Someone told Thomas Edison to give up after he had 283 failed attempts at the light bulb. "I can't stop now," said Edison. "I now know 283 ways not to do it. I am so close!"

When our teens experience a failure in life, we need to sit down together with them and discuss the lessons that can be received. They know they blew it, so there's no use in adding to their grief. If they can walk away with a positive view of failure, they will take more risks and receive more rewards in the future.

7. Teach A Positive Work Ethic.

When a teen comes home from school with an armful of homework, it's tempting to tell them to get as much done as they can. Our employers rarely tell us that. They tell us to get everything done.

Help your teens without doing their work. Let them know that you are available if they need assistance, but you want them to come to you out of necessity, not laziness.

8. Provide Positive Materials.

Everyone knows that we become like our focus. If we focus on the negative, we become negative. If we focus on the positive, we become positive.

Put positive resources in the hand of your teen. For birthdays and Christmas give CDs with wholesome lyrics. Cut out newspaper articles and tape television programs for your teen that will create and enhance a positive attitude.

9. Praise Positive Thoughts.

Teens hear a host of reasons why they cannot do certain things. "Wait until you're older." "I don't know them well enough." We all have our individual reasons as parents to say no at times. But when an opportunity arrives to say "Yes" say it with enthusiasm. Down play the "no,s" and draw attention to the "yeses."

Make a brief list of things you have told your teen no about. Is there anything on that list you can grant permission for now? If so, then surprise your teen with an unexpected, "Yes!"

10. Be Positive About Their Ideas.

As your ability to communicate as a family increases, so will each member's role in decision-making. Take into consideration the ideas your teen presents without belittling them. Showing interest in an idea does not mean you have to use it. In a family it's often more important to know we are heard and understood than to get our way. Make it a point to listen to their idea the same way you want someone to listen to yours.

Dear Parents,

We live in a world filled with negativism. It's everywhere at work, school play and, yes, even at church. Changing this worldly attitude starts at home. Homes should be safe places for our teens where they are encouraged and loved unconditionally. That doesn't mean that we overlook their faults, but that we train in love. Teens are at a vulnerable time in their lives when they are trying to find out who they really are. They should be allowed to fail and learn from their experiences. Teens (and people of all ages) are sometimes afraid that they won't measure up, so why try? This is where we as parents can help to encourage rather than discourage. Sometimes this can be hard when you come home after that long day at work and confront a problem with your teenager. This is definitely a time to think and pray before you speak. A word that tears down is very hard to take back. Proverbs 15:4 says "the tongue that brings healing is a tree of life, but a deceitful tongue crushes the spirit."

Hebrews 3:13 says that we are to encourage one another daily. In our family, we try to compliment as much as possible, especially the little things. Everyone in the family has responsibilities. For example, our youngest son is responsible for emptying the trash and the recycle and our oldest son has yard duty. We always make it a point to compliment them on their normal responsibilities as well as those special times when they do exceptionally well (like doing their chores without being reminded). You must make a conscious effort to do this. This is so important because they will mess up, and when correction is needed they need to know they were and still are loved.

Pray for your children daily and ask God to help you to find those things in which to praise your teen. Be careful what you say and how you say it. Body language can sometimes be as strong as your words. Your son may walk in the room with those baggy pants that you absolutely can't stand, but he is wearing a great looking belt to keep them in place. What will your response be? Hold your tongue and take a deep breath until you can meet the situation positively. We're not saying lower your standards, but try to remember what is really important. Is it your relationship or the pants? What were you wearing when you were a teen? Somehow you managed to regain your brain after your teen years. Give your teen the same benefit of the doubt.

People who came to Jesus always found encouragement because He accepted them. He didn't accept their sin, but He loved them anyway. Find positive ways to love and encourage your teen. Pray with them, study with them and let them know you love them no matter what.

Doug & Janet Morrison

Chapter 5

10 Tips For Disciplining Adolescents

1. Establish Family Rules.

As parents we can handle each problem as it arises or we can set rules and try to avoid some problems. It is impossible for us to have a rule for every imaginable circumstance, but we can set standards for problems we know we are going to encounter such as curfew, and dating age.

Establish the house rules as early as you can. When a teen at 16 tries to break a rule in existence since age 13, ignorance can't be an excuse.

2. Make Sure The Rules Are Understood By Your Teen.

Setting vague, or easily manipulated rules do little good. Maintain eye contact and get a verbal response from your teen to be positive that he or she understands the rules.

You may want to consider a commitment contract. Write down your rules, go over them as a family, and have each member sign the contract agreeing that they understand and will abide by the rules.

3. Explain The Consequences Of Breaking The Rules.

At most quick stops you will find a sign similar to, "IF YOU ROB THIS STORE YOU WILL RECEIVE A MINIMUM OF 20 YEARS IN PRISON." The message is simple, understandable, and the consequences are clear. The same should be true in our homes.

When the rules have been set, have your teen help you decide the consequences. You may decide together that a late curfew will mean not going out next weekend. This is also a learning process for your teen because they will be faced with similar situations when they have children.

4. Balance Punishment With Praise.

Do our teens feel like we are constantly getting on to them? Although we are trying to shape their character, we need to remember that praise shapes better than punishment.

For one month keep a list of every good word or deed that you notice about your child. At the end of the month write a letter thanking him or her for the great example, and then list all the things you wrote down over the month.

5. Do Not Compromise The Rules.

If you formed and signed a family contract it will be easy to review the rules and stand by them without giving in. When a teen says, "I hate you," or the tears start flowing there will be a temptation to let their bad behavior slide— don't. Businesses or lawyers do not compromise on signed contracts. You may make a new contract for the next need, but do not back down on the one that is in effect now.

6. Learn From Your Past Parenting Mistakes.

As parents we make many mistakes while trying to get our teens to the independent stage of their lives. Children do not come with instructions, and we raise them with a lot of trial and error. Learning from the errors of the past will help prevent errors in the future.

Meet with others parents of teens and discuss the mistakes we all have made and what we have learned. You may want to make notes physically or mentally to help prepare for upcoming parenting issues.

7. Seek Advice From Others.

Our pride often prevents us from reaching out and asking for help. We want to come across as ideal parents, and we don't want to look like we don't know what to do with our kids. But there is no shame in seeking assistance. It is better to lower our pride so we can become stronger parents than to remain prideful and hurt our families.

Delve into a variety of sources for advice. Books, friends, doctors, and counselors all offer a different, but valuable, perspective.

8. Use Teachable Moments.

A teachable moment can be any event, conversation, television program, etc., that allows you to point to a principle that can develop character, understanding, or maturity in your teen. For example, you may be reading the paper one morning and an article discusses the pregnancy rate among teenagers. Ask for your teen's opinion and start a discussion.

Some of the best teachable moments come when you share some of the struggles you faced as a young person. Use this tip as a tool to prevent discipline.

9. Discipline Differently When Necessary.

If you have more than one teen in the home, you will probably have more than one personality. As you probably know, there are homes who have one teen who is the greatest kind of person and one who may be considered the "black sheep."

While you want to use the same level of discipline, every form of shaping children does not work the same for each child. Take into consideration personality, and individual traits when setting the type of disciplinary measure. This is where contracts for the individual child can be developed.

10. Show And Tell Your Love For Them.

I used to think my mom was lying when she said, "I'm only doing this because I love you." With kids of my own, I realize she was honest.

Never punish your teen without expressing your love. They may not believe you, and may think to themselves that they despise you, but your years of showing your love through discipline and verbally saying, "I love you" will be a seed that will bloom in adulthood.

Dear Parents,

We would like to share some thoughts with you concerning the experiences we've had in raising our two children. Jason, our oldest at 27, is a third year medical student at St. Georges University School of Medicine in Grenada, West Indies. He currently is doing his clinical rotations in New York City. Haley, our youngest, is 15. Within just a few weeks she will be a 10th grader. Yes, your math is right. There is 12 years between them. That's been one of the adventures in parenting! Not only is there the difference in male and female, but also there is the age spread, the personality differences, and the fact that mom and dad are a little older now than when our first child came along. Obviously, what worked well with Jason hasn't always worked as well with Haley. We, as parents, had to relearn some parenting skills and acquire some new ones we didn't have, and, still we have much to learn. We have made some mistakes. But through it all God has blessed us with two wonderful, Christian children.

Here are some suggestions we would make regarding some of the things we've learned which will help in the area of disciplining. First, we have come to understand that every child is different. That's not a problem; it's the way God made us. But we make a mistake by assuming that you can treat every child the same. Get to know your children as individuals. Second, really listen to your children. Our children know when we are not really listening to them. We may be distracted or busy when they try to talk to us and we often pretend to be listening, but they know the difference. Third, always accentuate the positive in your children. Instead of pointing out the negatives or the mistakes they make, try to always point out the positive things they do. One of us has had difficulty with this one and our youngest constantly reminds us that we tend to overlook the positive and focus only on the negative. It will make a difference! Fourth, don't make mountains out of molehills. There will be enough mountains without our creating others unnecessarily. Work on not overreacting to things that might just be normal adolescent behavior. Fifth, spend time with your children. There is no substitute for being together in a variety of activities. Time together is where you build understanding. Sixth, set the spiritual tone of your household. Let your children see and know that spiritual matters are of utmost importance in your home. Seventh, let your children see that you, as husband and wife, love each other. The fear of divorce is high in children when

36

they see much arguing and disagreement between spouses. There will be times of disagreement in every marriage, but be sure to let them see and hear that you love each other. Eighth, reward your children with additional trust when they have proven themselves trustworthy. Your children will respond positively because they begin to understand that reward comes from positive behavior and that punishment comes from negative behavior and when trust is broken. Ninth, don't be afraid to set boundaries. Actually, our experience has been that boundaries and limits have been appreciated and have given "safe haven" to our children many times. It takes a lot of pressure off them and decisions that they sometimes are compelled to make without the wisdom and experience of age. And finally, tenth, we can make many mistakes as parents, and get away with it, if our children know that we love them unconditionally and with all our hearts.

In Christian Love,
Howard & Donna Todd

10 Tips For Family Communication

1. Learn To Listen Attentively.

It has often been said that God gave us one mouth and two ears so we could listen twice as much as we talk. The Lord puts it like this, "Be slow to speak and quick to listen."

Before you say, "Now you listen to me, young lady," hear your teen's side of the story. Let him or her have a complete say so you can speak clearly and respond to the details appropriately.

2. Be Consistent.

Consistency in communication patterns will help open the gate to your teen's heart. If we scream one time, and are pleasant the next, they won't know what to expect. That type of temperament will drive a teen to silence.

If you struggle with consistency, chart your communication pattern. On a sheet of graph paper place the #1 on a low line and the #10 on a high line. "1" = calm. "10" = volcanic. Keep a record for three months, then evaluate and make any needed corrections.

3. Remove Distractions.

Close the book, turn off the television, fold up the newspaper and take care of any other distraction so you can give full attention to your teen. When we refuse to focus on the conversation our children perceive us as uninterested. Once we establish that thought in their minds, it will be difficult to change the attitude.

Make it obvious that you want to listen. Say, "Hold on a minute, honey. Let me turn off the radio, I don't want to miss a word."

4. Ask Relevant Questions.

A paraphrase of James 4:2 might read, "You do not

know because you do not ask." Teens rarely volunteer information, but with the right questions and the right approach you can discover a multitude of tidbits.

Use caution. You don't want to come across as prying, or intrusive. Start with shallow questions and work deeper as the teen opens up.

5. Confront With Gentleness.

A quick way to destroy communication is to jump all over a teen before a conversation gets started. We expect our teens to stand there and take it while we verbally pound on them. They may stand there, but inside they are not taking it well at all.

You can be gentle and firm at the same time. Use a strong but soft tone to communicate seriousness and care.

6. Be Willing To Apologize.

How many times have we said, "I shouldn't have to apologize! It's their fault I lost my temper!" Justifying our mistakes, or placing the blame on our children for the wrong only weakens family communication.

Say, "I'm sorry" as soon as possible. If we want teens to "fess up" when they blow it, they first need to see it modeled through our lives.

7. Communicate On Their Level.

Most of us would find it difficult to talk to a mechanic about rebuilding a transmission. Why? Because we know nothing about it. Our teens find it difficult to talk to us when we know nothing about their world. Stay up-to-date with the latest music, movies, and teen idols. Be current without trying too hard to be cool, though, or you'll risk becoming even more "lame" to your teen than you are already.

Show interest in your teen's passions. Purchase a book or CD that you know is by a favorite author or artist. Use the gift as an opportunity to talk about the interest.

8. Use Correct Body Language.

Eye contact signals attentiveness. A nod of the head says "I'm with you." Folded arms communicate, "Keep talking, I can't wait to get my turn." Statistics show that over

80% of communication takes place through body language.

Concentration not only on your body talk, but your teen's as well without drawing attention to what you notice. "Don't roll your eyes at me!" will make a teen shut down. Instead, recognize the resistance and take an alternate approach.

9. Use Touch To Affirm When Words Won't Work.

Terms become useless in certain situations, such as the death of a friend, a break-up, or failing to make the team. In those moments give a hug, pat on the back, or other touches that say, "I care" without saying a word.

Don't limit touch to hurtful times. After a win or a great test score, serve a gigantic bear hug to your teen (but wait till you get home or the embarrassment will kill the effect).

10. Close All Communication With Love.

Regardless of the conversation, or the circumstances thereof, close with love. Let "I love you" be the last words your teen hears at the end of every time together.

Say, "I love you" at least ten times a day, and for no apparent reason. Don't reserve these three words for special occasions but allow them to flow freely at all times.

Dear Parents,

Since the day our daughter was born (she's now 16) our mornings begin with a prayer of thanksgiving for this child and for guidance in raising her.

In deciding what we wanted for our child we felt that communication was very important. From the first day of her life we have set a time each day to talk. We talk about events of the day, plans we have, and about special people in her life. At her early age she would respond with smiles and coos; and as she was able to talk she would also share the events of her day. I worked outside of home and when I picked her up from daycare she would get into the car talking about her day. We talked about her friends and teachers. If she had a special story to tell me, such as a friend not being nice to her, I would use this opportunity to explain kindness, sharing honesty (such as telling the truth to her teacher!) and whatever else related to her story. This practice has carried on into her school life.

A lot of our conversations about the day's events take place at the dinner table with her dad and me. She has told some real "eye opening" stories about what she has seen and heard. We always listen and we discuss these situations. We don't always like what we hear, but we use these times to explain our views and beliefs and listen to hers. She knows there is nothing she cannot tell us.

We are involved in all her activities. We attend school meetings and parent meetings. We attend any assembly or performance that she is in. We attend church together. We know her teachers, her principals, her instructors, her friends, her friends' parents, her boyfriends, her employers, and they know us.

Abbie never goes to bed thinking we are angry with her. She never leaves the house or hangs up the phone when she has called from out of town without hearing the words "I love you."

And those words are spoken with the deepest meaning. Abbie knows we are proud of who she is and what she stands for.

Abbie is the center of our family and Christ is the center of our life. We are truly blessed.

Sincerely,
Bill and Peggy Butler

Chapter 7

10 Don'ts Of Communication

1. Don't Be Overly Critical.

Criticism has its place, but not when it is used in a destructive way. No one wants to be told about their imperfections without receiving a possible solution. No one likes to hear about his or her faults in a faultfinding tone. No one wants to talk with a person who only expresses the negative about us.

Practice favorable criticism with your teen. Identify the undesired behavior and offer a practical solution. Talk with them about the problem without becoming emotional.

2. Don't Interrupt.

"But Dad. If you would..." "Be quiet. I'll let you know when you can speak." Does that sound familiar? If so, think back to the time when your parents cut you off in the middle of a sentence. How did it make you feel? Possibly the same as your teen.

Let your kids finish their thoughts completely without interrupting or giving your rebuttal. You may disagree. You may even get angry, but let them finish.

3. Don't Lose Your Temper.

Anger only hinders communication and forces both sides to express unfiltered thoughts. We have all said things under the influence of fury that we wish we could take back five seconds later.

"In your anger do not sin: Do not let the sun go down while you are still angry" Ephesians 4:26. When both of you lose your temper, don't go to bed without a resolution.

4. Don't Use Sarcasm.

Sarcasm means to "rip away the flesh." That's a powerful picture of what happens when we use our tongue to cut someone. Witty comebacks and put downs may seem cute, but they're cutting to teens. Their self-image is already sagging and sarcasm only deepens their self-doubt.

Make a conscious decision not to say anything that will put down instead of build up. When you feel a divisive word coming on, stop and consider the impact.

5. Don't Dwell On the Past.

When a teen makes a mistake in life, especially a major mistake, it is hard for us not to use it as a weapon. If they know that we are going to dig up the past during a conversation, teens will avoid communication and us.

Mention the past only as a tool to remind your teen of a previous lesson learned. If you see a mistake about to repeat itself, refresh the memory of your child about the previous negative results.

6. Don't Nag.

Parental DNA must contain a nagging gene because it is so natural for us. We are not trying to be irritating, we just want to be clear, so we repeat ourselves about 10,000 times. For some odd reason this gets on our teen's nerves - go figure.

When a teen says, "Okay! I've got it," let it go. If they really don't have it, the failure will be a learning experience. If they do, you've learned how to communicate without nagging.

7. Don't Lecture.

This form of one-sided communication let's parents feel like they had their say even though their teen tuned out halfway through the first sentence. Lecturing suggests an "I'm right, you're wrong" attitude.

Facilitate communication by asking questions and getting feedback during your sit down discussion. You may have ten critical items to cover, but a lecture will not enhance mental absorption; open sharing will.

8. Don't Threaten.

"If you do that one more time, you will not leave this house for a year." Really? An entire year? Well, if you say it, you must follow through or your teen will question every punishment ever mentioned. Look back at the consequences listed on your contract and see what the punishment is for what just happened.

Prepare the punishment ahead of time. There is no way to predict every problem, but we can be ready for some. Plan ahead by promising yourself to never make rash or exaggerated threats. Consider a fair discipline and have it ready for the unexpected.

9. Don't Lie.

To keep from looking foolish to our family, we sometimes think it's better to lie than tell the truth. Once the truth is discovered, we have compromised our integrity and the inroads we've made in family conversation.

Tell the truth (Be sure of your position). The whole truth (Don't leave out portions to suit your needs). And nothing but the truth (Don't add anything to embellish your words).

10. Don't Force Communication.

Sometimes silence is the best correspondence. Anger, remorse, pain, or other emotions may call for quietness. There will be a time for words of correction or support. Until then, let your teens have time to digest their feelings before beginning a discussion.

Give your teen an open invitation to conversation with you. Let him or her know that you are ready to talk when the time is right. That may be a few hours or a day. When your teen doesn't want to talk, use immediate conversation only in especially trying situations.

Dear Parents,

Everyone knows how important it is to keep the communication lines open between parents and children. We are inundated with information regarding how to talk, what to talk about, and when to talk to our children. But even when you follow all the directions, sometimes it is not enough.

We are the parents of four children, now all in their twenties. As they were growing up we smugly thought that we were doing a pretty good job communicating with our children. We always tried to create an open environment in which the kids would feel comfortable talking to us about anything. Our children were always told that they could come to us with any problem that they had. We discussed sensitive subjects over dinner, and by example let them know that no subject was off limits with the family. Anything they wanted to talk over, we did. What we weren't as successful in, however, was setting the right example of communication for our children. It is so true that children do as they see their parents do.

Our family was a very private family. On the outside, we looked perfect. Everyone always commented what a great family we were. We felt that the only way to be accepted was to look good on the outside and keep all of our problems to ourselves. Therefore, no matter what our family was going through, we didn't talk about it to outsiders, and especially not to members of the church. We see now that our children followed our footsteps: if you have something potentially harmful to your image, keep it to yourself.

Through several crises that occurred when our children were in their teens, we as parents learned that no man (or family) is an island. We found that our children did not talk to us about everything; in fact, there were many revelations as time passed that we didn't have a clue about. Some of our teens covered up embarrassing mistakes that they had made until it was too late to even TRY to correct them. They got deeper and deeper into their problems, but didn't turn to us in their times of greatest need. After all, we wanted everyone to know what a good family we were.

We discovered through God and with the assistance of the church that we can only make it through a relationship with God and the friendship of others. When we began opening up to others, especially our church friends, about our problems, things began improving dramatically.

If we could change anything about those teenage years, we would definitely ask specific questions about our children's lives. It isn't enough to invite them to talk to you.

Don't give up,
Terry and Cindy Williams

46

Chapter 8

10 Tips For Family Meetings

1. Choose A Convenient Time.

Finding a time when the entire family can be together may take a combination of sacrifice and commitment. Even thirteen-year-olds seem to have a schedule that keeps them busy every hour of the day.

Ask each family member to turn in a schedule of their average week. Look it over and pinpoint the times when a majority of the household does not have conflicting events and plan to meet during one of those times.

2. Set A Maximum Meeting Length.

Make the meetings short and precise. If discussion carries the meeting over the prescribed time that's fine, but covering a list of unimportant material will only make further meetings dreaded.

Cover everything that touches each family member early in the meeting. If your allotted time is one hour, save anything that would not specifically include the children until last and let them leave after the set time.

3. Cover The Meeting With Prayer.

Philippians 4:6 says, "Worry about nothing, pray about everything." Begin and close every time together by talking to the Father. Take prayer requests and mention each individual during the prayer time.

Rely on spontaneous prayer during the meeting. If a family member mentions a problem or shares a need, stop and pray.

4. Choose The Right Place.

The couch is comfortable enough to promote snoozing, while the table is rigid enough to close discussion. Decide on a location that will be free from distractions or interruptions. You may choose to sit on the floor to aid intimacy, or sit in a circle of chairs to give the feeling of community.

Whatever place your family chooses, require the following: Turn off all televisions, radios, beepers, and phones, cellular or otherwise. Turn on the answering machine with the volume all the way down.

5. Make The Meeting Relevant.

What will be your target for the meeting? Just getting together and asking, "So what do you guys want to talk about?" isn't going to help anyone enjoy the time.

Weeks before the meeting ask each family member to make a list of things they feel you need to discuss. A teen might have some questions about the prom. A parent might want some ideas about a summer vacation.

6. Allow Each Person Ample Time To Speak.

This is a *family meeting*, not a parents meeting. Set a ground rule that refuses to allow anyone to dominate the conversation. Not giving others an opportunity to share will make them think the meeting is only about your agenda.

This is a little rigid, but if someone continues to take over and start a long breathless lecture, you may put him or her on the clock. Provide two minutes of talk time for that member, then move on.

7. Don't Interrupt.

Just don't do it. It's rude. Period. End of sentence.

8. Consider The Feelings And Opinions Of Others With out Judging.

Considering does not mean you accept or agree with their feelings or position. It does communicate that you care. We all have a need to be heard without others jumping to conclusions.

If a feeling or opinion is shared that does not correlate with Scripture or the values of the family, explore the issue without passing sentence until the details are known.

9. Break The Rules Occasionally.

After a few meetings the family will feel like they can predict the format. Without telling anyone, make an announcement when you all get together, "Tonight our family meeting will be held at the Ice-Cream Castle!" Leave immediately and have a great time.

If needed, share light family matters while you eat. If a stronger issue comes up, put it aside and discuss it when you get home.

10. Brag Session.

Use part of the meeting time to share something fantastic about each other. Talk about what you appreciate. Relive favorite family memories. Build each other up. Don't hold back. Now is your chance to make everyone in the family feel great.

Brag Bag. Give each person a small piece of paper to write his or her name. Place all the names in the bag and draw. The name you pick is the person you brag about.

Dear Parents,

There have been a lot of family meetings in the Newman home. Mom stays at home. Dad works close to home. Our five children are schooled in our home. This has been the case for over ten years. And for most of those years, the television has been absent from our home. In addition, we chose not to participate in many church activities, especially those that divide and segregate the family. So there has been a lot of time for family meetings, both informal and formal.

The informal meetings usually take place at meal time. At our house, this means an average of two meetings per day. These meetings allow for open discussions. Often our discussions float from one topic to another quickly as everyone seems to have different priorities at times, but all get a chance to speak and all are encouraged to speak, one at a time. It allows our family to talk about things they think are important.

The formal meetings occur in the morning and evening, and sometimes at noon. They are in the form of devotions. They are formal in the sense that Scripture is read and undivided attention is expected. These meetings are especially fruitful, because no Scripture is eliminated from discussion. The Bible is simply read through, some from Proverbs in the morning, a certain book of interest at noon if we meet then, and a New Testament reading in the evening. This allows our family to talk about things that God thinks are important.

So, in our opinion, family meetings are more than important, they are essential. They help our family know and imitate Jesus Christ.

Following Him,
Joe & Debbie Newman

Chapter 9

10 Secrets Teens Want Their Parents To Know

1. Teens Want Their Parents To Know They Love Them.

It is difficult for some teens to express their love for their parents. For whatever reason, showing affection or telling their parents about their love for them is very uncomfortable.

Continually express your love for your teens so they will know their statements or acts of love will not be rejected.

2. Teens Want To Discover Themselves.

"Who am I?" and "What is my place in this world?" are universal questions. Because of the rapid changes emotionally, physically, and spiritually, teens feel it is critical to make their mark on their world.

Encourage teens to make their mark while helping them realize that life is made up of multiple marks. No single moment defines a person's life. Help create a vision that says each day holds the possibility of further self-discovery for God's glory.

3. Teens Want To Feel Needed.

They want to know their ideas are important, and that their input is relevant to the family. Teens desire to feel that they are making a contribution.

Supply opportunities beyond typical chores for teens to feel needed. If your teen is a web surfing professional, let him or her do the research for an upcoming trip. If he or she just got a driver's license, send him or her on a special mission.

4. Teens Want To Be Disciplined.

Can we really believe that teens want to have limits? Maybe they don't want to be told to be in by 10 p.m., but they do want what a standard communicates, which is, "I care about you and love you, so for your own good you have got to be in by this time."

Provide a reason for the restriction. Discipline only to show authority breeds resentment and rebellion. Discipline for the sake of protection and betterment helps create long-term respect.

5. Teens Want To Be Respected.

We all know that respect is something to be earned through actions and character. Teens can feel that their young adulthood automatically qualifies them for the respect of others. They want to be respected for their decisions as well as their differences of opinion.

Grant regard for your teen in the areas where they have displayed trustworthiness. As you give a certain privilege or honor a decision, let him or her know that it relates to the way they have shown responsibility. This will teach teens that respect is not as difficult to earn as they once thought.

6. Teens Want To Show Appreciation On Their Own Terms.

When was the last time you heard "Thank you" from your teen for the food and shelter you provide? With the limited thanks we receive it is tempting to think teens don't care about what they have, but if you ask them what they are thankful for, our names and what we provide will be on the list.

Take the "yum" at the dinner table, and the "fun" as a sign of appreciation. Those grunts don't sound like much, but sometimes we need to take the smallest gesture and recognize the large statement it is coming from a teenager.

7. Teens Want To Follow Their Dreams, Not Our Dreams.

I clearly remember hiding my football uniform in a large garbage bag to keep from playing. My family wanted me to play, but I didn't want to. Whether it's sports or academics, give your children permission to pursue their dreams. If you really feel directed about a certain endeavor for your teen, use encouragement without pressure.

Don't use God to force your child into a particular area. For example, "The Lord gave you such a tremendous gift, it would be a sin not to use it."

8. Teens Want To Be Trusted.

Trust, like respect, has to be earned. Because of their impatience, teens want to be trusted now without proving their trustworthiness.

Place the responsibility to trust on all family members. You may show that you trust your teen by allowing him or her to stay out an extra thirty minutes. They have to show they were trustworthy by being home on time.

9. Teens Want Their Parents To Like Their Friends.

A typical teen line is, "So what that he has long hair and tattoos, he's a good guy." The difference in our generations causes us to be suspicious of anyone who doesn't meet our standard.

Welcome all of your teen's friends with open arms. If you see anything that is questionable, ask your teen about it later without using an interrogative voice.

10. Teens Want To Be Teens.

Underneath all the power struggles, underneath all the hidden agendas and the need to be cool, they simply want to be teens. They want to wear their kind of clothes and hang out with their style of friends.

As long as they don't get involved with anything ungodly, let's let them be what they want.

Dear Parents,

I have the greatest parents in the world. If I had to name just one aspect of the relationship I have with my parents that makes it what it is today, that characteristic would definitely be friendship. Remember that teenagers are learning to be on their own, learning about responsibility and the adult world. Approach them as a best friend instead of an overbearing, nosy parent. The fact that I know beyond a shadow of a doubt that they love me and trust me and that I can trust them makes such a huge impact on our relationship. I know that I can come to my parents with anything and they'll listen. I know that my parents are on my side and that makes all the difference in the world. Communication is certainly key to any relationship, especially one between a parent and their teenager. Listen to your kids before you jump the gun and make assumptions. Most of the time the arguments and fights I get into with my parents are over misunderstandings and miscommunications.

I believe the most important part of our relationship is the common bond of Jesus Christ we have between us. Because of that bond, I know we are all working for the same thing. We have a common goal. And because of our own relationships with God, we've learned how to communicate, interact, and be the type of daughter and parents (Ephesians 6:1-4) that God calls us to be. May God bless you in your relationships with your children. I pray that you will have a great relationship with your teens.

Because of Christ
Kellie Segrest

10 Tips For Building A Healthy Family

1. Pray Together.

Prayer builds spiritual intimacy between you and God, and between you and your family. It establishes openness about our lives and the things we feel need God's personal touch. Praying together helps everyone see one another's hurts and thankfulness at the same time.

As you pray mention your teens individually so they can hear you praying for them. Pray about school, your relationship with them, future mates, etc.

2. Build Positive Memories.

We have all heard older people talk about the "good old days." They share about walking to school in the snow carrying a biscuit in a syrup can. They talk about how they eloped in a horse drawn carriage. All of those memories bring a smile to their faces.

Don't wait for the "good old days," make them the "good now days." Don't always wait for memories to happen, make them happen. Plan an impromptu excursion this week and begin building positive memories.

3. Enjoy Family Nights.

A minimum of once a month block out a day or a night and do something family specific. Play games, help each other with problems, or just "hang out." These events are usually dreaded by teens in the beginning. Make it great, and the dread will disappear.

Teens usually are not too thrilled about a family night, so make sure everyone agrees on what you decide to do (I know that's asking for a miracle.) You just don't want it to end up like one of those vacation movies where the entire family hates the idea except the dad.

4. Maximize The Moment.

Enjoy every minute you have together as a family. You may not always be able to plan a night when everyone is present, so make the most of drive time to the mall or a ballgame. Walk around the block together.

Maximize the meaningless moments. Fight the temptation to turn drive time or any other time into a deep conversation. Show your child that you can spend time together without an interrogation.

5. Defend Your Teen.

When teens are wrong they are wrong, but when they're right stand up for them. Young people get the impression that the adult world is out to discredit them. Show your support by being a biased parent when needed. If he was accused of being involved in an activity and it's false, stay strong. Be sure that the defense is justified.

6. Teach Don't Tell.

How many teenagers do you know who like to be told what to do? Telling comes across as force, while teaching is interpreted as helping.

Think before you preach and discover ways to teach. Instead of telling your teen to take out the trash, how could you teach him or her to do it? Could you motivate her by letting her know it displays thankfulness? Would it encourage him to learn that God made him strong so he could serve effectively?

7. Disciple Your Teen.

A disciple follows the example of the leader and seeks to emulate the lifestyle. Healthy families develop when parents share the responsibilities of the household and set an example for their children to follow.

Regularly evaluate yourself as a disciple. Are there areas where you have been too firm or too lax? Write down the areas of your teen's life that need the most attention and let your life lead.

8. Spiritual Guidance.

I cannot remember a morning of my teen years when the

Bible was not open across the table from me when I came to breakfast. Before Mom made the toast or poured the juice, she spent time with God.

Accept responsibility for your teen's spiritual development. The church, Christian education, devotionals and other activities only supplement what you provide in the home.

9. Model Financial Stewardship.

"I need some money," parts the pocketbooks of millions of parents a day. Debits and credits mean little to the average young person; they just see us as their money tree for the mall.

If it is not too personal, ask your teen to help you balance the checkbook. Let him or her see where the money goes and why each month can be so difficult. Show how the first part of your income goes to God and have your teen start doing the same with their money.

10. Get Physical.

Get your muscles pumping together as a family, and plan nutritious meals together.

Help hold each other accountable with your exercise program. Use it as an encouragement, not as a competition, and it will be one more thing that your family can have in common.

Dear Parents,

Raising children is an awesome responsibility, but certainly a great time in your life. God blessed us with two wonderful boys to mold into Christian young men and productive citizens. Raising children is no easy task and we certainly made some mistakes. I equate this with holding a bar of soap. If you hold the soap too tight, it will pop out. It you hold it too loosely, it will also pop out. You must hold it gently.

The most important thing that you can do is to take your children to church. Raise your children with a Christian family and Christian influences. Remember to have fun together as a family.

We always believed in consistent discipline-whether it be spanking or other methods. When the boys got older, they respected our authority and required less discipline. The example you set as parents means so much. Believe me, you will be observed and critiqued.

We always tried to encourage our boys in all their projects, interests, hobbies, and team sports. Their age difference was three years, so they were always on different teams, but we always found a way to be there.

There is no substitute for the love of a mother as she carried them before they were born. Janice protected these boys like a mother hen. Bill always provided food, clothing and shelter for us. This is the best example a father can pass on to his sons. We both told them often that we loved them.

From the time they were young and said their prayers before going to sleep and thanking God for their food, they were taught the wonderful gift of prayer. This is important later in life as they pray for other reasons.

Sometimes we allowed them to do things that we were not fully agreeable with. We didn't want to hold the soap too tight. They learned some valuable lessons which prove that experience is the best teacher. Realize that each child has his own personality and what works for one may not work for the other.

Going to a Christian private school also helps, but is no substitute for what we previously mentioned. By no means did we do a perfect job. Neither did our parents and neither will you. Transferring the good values of our parents to our children to build their character is very important. Now as both of our sons will be bringing children into the world this year, we become grandparents who reinforce all the good values that make having families fun.

In Christian love,
Bill and Janice Pemberton

Chapter 11

10 Questions Parents Need To Ask Their Teens

1. "How Is Your Relationship With God?"

Listen for terms of intimacy and maturity. You may discover that your teen has your faith and not a personal faith.

Ask your teen to share the ways they grow closer to the Lord. Find out about quiet time and prayer habits. Of course the biggest testament to the relationship with God will be a Christ-like lifestyle.

2. "How Are We Doing As A Family?"

On the one hand, they can respond, "Wonderful. There cannot be a better family than ours." On the other hand, teens might say, "Our family is a living definition of dysfunction."

Give complete permission for your teen to express himself without reservation. We ask these questions so we can become better parents, so the truth will always be more helpful than a lie. If your teen says that you are a dysfunctional parent then, give them a chance to explain.

3. "Who Are Your Friends?"

Recently, Gene Stallings visited our congregation and on the subject of parenting he said, "If a parent doesn't know the names of their children's friends, they don't know their children."

Get to know more than names. Get to *know* your children's friends. Ask about their interests, about their parents, and about their faith. You might even want to get their names, addresses, and phone numbers just in case you need to reach them, your teen, or their parents.

4. "What Can I Do To Help You?"

Most of the time you will get an answer like, "I'm okay" or "Nothing." It probably seems like a waste of time to ask such a question, and right now that may be true. Your thoughtfulness, however, will be remembered and one day they may reward your genuine concern with a way you can help.

Keep asking. It can be tiring to hear "nothing" or even worse, "Just leaving me alone would be a big help," but hang on. Your persistence will prove your love.

5. "Why Do You Listen To That Kind Of Music?"

Give your teen a chance to explain why he or she chooses a particular style of music. For some it's the message, for others it's the beat, and for most of us it's terrifying. Ask your teen "What are they saying" in those lyrics?

Listen to your teen's music together. If it is Godly there won't be a problem. If it's not, you'll hear every possible excuse concerning why you don't need to listen.

6. "How Do You Feel You Contribute To This Family?"

This is not a trick question. Teens often view themselves as dispensable, so let them see how critical they are to your family unit by using this question.

Your teen may not be able to think of an answer and that can leave him or her feeling worthless. Prepare a list of ways that you know your teen makes a positive impact on the family and if "I don't know" is the answer; you will be ready to prove their worth.

7. "How Are Things Going At School?"

Ask about teachers, assignments, friends (by name if possible), and upcoming events. Stay informed about school situations by letting your teen be the "source."

What are the odds of your teen telling you everything about school? Attend meetings, get the school newspaper, and become a friendly parent to the principal. Use these contacts as a way to ask specific questions about school, but avoid sounding like a detective.

8. "What Does Our Family Do For You?"

Encourage your teen to be more expressive than stating the obvious like food and shelter. Ask about the family's impact on them emotionally, spiritually, and physically.

We should never ask this question when we are trying to prove to teens that they really have it good. Use this, and the other questions, in tension-free moments - as few as they may be.

9. "If You Could Change One Thing About Our Family, What Would It Be?"

Get ready, you asked for it. Do you really want to know? Listen with an open mind and heart because this dangerous question may hold the key to taking your family to the next level in life.

Take the answer seriously and look for ways to make it a reality if it is possible.

10. "If You Were Me, What Would You Do?"

This is a great question to ask if you are in conflict. It places the burden of responsibility on teens and forces them to look from another angle. It may help them change their mind about a decision, or their answer may help you change your mind.

Don't wait for a problem before using this technique. Get a book like *Tension Getters* (available from Youth Specialties) and place your teens in different fictional situations to see how they would respond to a given situation.

Dear Parents,

Communicating with our teenager is really no different than communicating with each other. You cannot expect to have an open door to communication with him or her if you are constantly slamming the door shut with angry outbursts. Learning not to overreact is a must. Learning to take a step back and seriously think about whether or not this is really a BIG issue is very important. Walk away if you must to give yourself time to cool down and think. We expect them not to have angry outbursts. Why should we be any different? Ask yourself, "Is his behavior or what he is asking to do in line with the Christian principles you are wanting your family to follow?" If it is not a moral issue, it may be time to step back and let this one go in exchange for his attention on more weighty matters. Tell your child that you do not like _____, but you will not interfere as long as he agrees to listen when you really do need to interfere. You will be giving him some space and earning his respect.

Communication cannot take place at the wrong time or in the wrong location. Drilling your daughter with questions on the way home from school or when she has just walked in the door from a party will not net a whole lot of information. One problem families have today is that they are just not spending much time alone together. We may be spending time together on the baseball field or at church, but that is not the same as spending one on one time alone with each child. While family meal time is one way to spend time talking to each other, the best time to communicate with your child comes when you are engaged in some activity together –alone. It is much easier for him or her to slide in a question of greater importance while raking the yard with you or shopping.

Finally, launching off into yet another preaching episode simply will not work. Your sermon will go in one ear and out the other. The teenage years are years when you should practice what you preach instead of preaching about what you hope you practice. Live it and they will learn it.

Only with His help,
Wendell & Billie Scroggins

Chapter 12

10 Tips For Overcoming Parental Discouragements

1. Realize You Are Not Alone.

Teenagers can say and do things that will make you feel like you have taught them nothing. Oddly, when we go through a storm we feel that the sun is shining on everyone but us. The truth is that the rain that drenches your life, drenches the life of your neighbor as well.

Turn to others who have raised teens or are raising them now and you will find a kindred spirit. Pool the wisdom of your experiences and become encouragement to one another.

2. Serve Others.

Jesus said, "The Son of Man came to serve, not to be served" (Mark 10:45). When our eyes are on others we lose track of ourselves. Focusing on our problems leads to being consumed by them. If there is nothing practical we can do at the moment to meet a parental challenge, serving others will present a way to rest from the circumstances and produce something of purpose.

Contact your Chamber of Commerce or your local school and ask for a list of organizations in your community that accept volunteer assistance. Choose one close to your heart, get involved, and receive the joy that comes from serving.

3. Repeat God's Promises Often.

When discouragement overwhelms you turn to the One who never fails. Consider Proverbs 6:20b, "Do not forsake your mother's teaching" and ask, "What would Mom do at this time?" Or how about Romans 14:19, "...do what leads to peace and mutual edification" and put into action some ways you can make that real in your home.

Don't wait until you are discouraged to remember God's vows to you. Claim them during the calm moments to help prevent the rough ones.

4. Confide In A Friend.

This may or may not be another parent. Who is the one person you can trust above all others? Write his or her name here _____. Whenever you begin to feel discouraged pick up the phone, or email your friend and share your burden.

Be specific when you call. Be upfront about your reason for dialing their number. Making them drag the problem out of you will only aggravate your friend and make you feel guiltier about the call. Make sure that these conversations are confidential unless it is life threatening.

5. Keep A Journal.

Journal is an adult name for a diary. Use it as a tool to chronicle your life. Through the years you will be able to reflect on the good and bad times and determine their true effect on your life after you are distanced from the situation.

Combine journaling with your daily quiet time. Many of the best reflections of life will come after you have reflected on Scripture. *My Utmost for His Highest* by Oswald Chambers is one of the most popular. If you are not sure about which one to choose, ask your local Christian bookstore.

6. Beat Self-Pity.

Counting your curses instead of the blessings has never led to encouragement. When discouraged, beat self-pity by counting your blessings and realizing just how rich you are compared to most of the world. Did you know that if you live in America you are in the wealthiest 3% in the world?

Keep a blessing list posted on your refrigerator. Have each family member's name on it and space for them to write their blessings. Once a day walk by and review your blessings list.

7. Be Optimistic.

Zig Ziglar, world recognized optimist, says, "It's not where you start - it's where you finish that counts." Pessimism saturates our society, so there is no need to add to the overflow.

Talk to positive people and ask them how they are able see the good in bad situations. When you feel a negative spell coming on, give them a call and ask them how they would view the situation.

8. Get Plenty Of Rest.

Physiologically and psychologically we cannot function properly without the required amount of rest. That translates into depression and discouragement concerning areas that would be no big deal any other time.

Schedule rest. We make appointments for work, play, and doctor's visits, so why not rest. Put yourself on schedule and parenting will become less stressful even when your teen comes in an hour late.

9. Join A Support Group.

#1 called for remembering that you're not alone. A support group for parents of teens provides a place where all in the room will know they are wrestling with similar challenges.

If your congregation does not offer such groups call others in your area. If no churches do, pray about starting one yourself.

10. Remember: Blessings Follow Burdens.

Read chapter 39 of Genesis. Joseph had it tough and it didn't look like there was much hope. But after chapter 39 is chapter 40 where Joseph became number two in the kingdom!

Remind yourself daily that Christ's burden became your blessing.

Dear Parents,

Jesus said "in Me you may have peace. In this world you will have trouble. But take heart! I have overcome the world." (John 16:33 NIV). As Pat and I raised our three kids we often wondered if Jesus or anybody else ever really understood. It was not only difficult, frustrating, and discouraging, but it seemed the harder we tried to do the 'right thing', the harder the world was teaching our kids the 'wrong thing'. There were times when we were just about ready to give up, just about ready to throw in the towel and let the world have its way. But we didn't, and I am glad we didn't.

But understand our kids didn't turn out perfect. Nor did they turn out anywhere near what we envisioned as we were raising them. There were, and still are, heartaches, frustrations, and discouragement. But that's life. In the world there is "trouble" and it will always be this way. Our job as parents is not to correct all the problems of the world, but to do the best we can in 'our' world. My dad once told me that my job as a father was to try and do a little better job with my kids than he had done with me. So Pat and I have simply done our best with what God has given us and trusted Him to produce the results He wants.

In 1963, at the ripe old age of 17, I informed my parents that I was going to quit high school, get a job, and marry my girlfriend. I had it all figured out: work 8 to 5 somewhere, come home and spend blissful hours with my 'woman'. Of course my mother went ballistic, but finally gave in and said okay. I promptly announced my decision and started looking for the perfect job. Three days later I was back in school being a teenager again. Years later Mom shared with me the anguish and advice that produced the decision to say yes...I had discussed my intentions with our school counselor. My mother went to that counselor to get her to talk me out of this madness. But instead the counselor told my mother to let me go. She told my mom, "all my training and experience tells me that John will not go very far. You and Mr. Tew have done a good job raising him, it is now time to let him make his own mistakes." Amid many tears my parents let me go, and right on cue I came right back.

Here is the lesson. Do the best you can and then let go. Trust God, trust yourself, but most of all, trust your kids. You are not perfect, and they will not be perfect. Never give up, but never be afraid to let go.

Loving Him,
John and Pat Tew

Chapter 13

10 Tips To Teach Teens About Finances

1. Give The First 10% To God.

You don't have to limit your family to ten percent. The key is that your giving is sacrificial. King David said, "I will not sacrifice to the LORD my God burnt offerings that cost me nothing."

Get an envelope and write "God's Money" on it. Hand it to your teen and challenge him or her to put the first ten percent of allowance or work money in the envelope, then give it during the offering.

2. Save 10%.

Dedicate the next ten percent of income to savings. Get separate envelopes or a ledger and list all the items you need to save for (car insurance, clothes, entertainment, etc.)

Take your teen to the bank and open a savings account. Every time some money is acquired go to the bank and make the deposit.

3. Invest 10%.

Teaching teens to invest will help them plan for their future. They may need to invest for college, or for retirement. By teaching this principle early in their lives we can help instill a habit that will bless their families in years to come.

Make an appointment to meet with a financial counselor or an investment broker to help your teen see the importance of starting young. Their motivation will be enhanced when they witness the power of compounding interest from someone who knows about money.

4. Live Off 70%.

After giving to God, saving, and investing only seventy percent remains. Because of poor financial decisions most of us feel that it impossible to live off such an amount. If we are wise with God's money, the majority in America can flourish with such a sum.

Train your teen to budget and to know where every cent goes. If you are not currently budgeting, you can learn this process together. Larry Burkett's organization, Christian Financial Concepts, can provide any materials you may need to get your family on the right financial track.

5. Eliminate Debts.

"Let no debt remain outstanding..." (Romans 13:8). One of the primary sources of debt is the use of credit, and credit cards. It seems so convenient to pay over time and get now what you can pay for later. If you choose to carry a credit card, use one like American Express, which requires you to pay the balance each month.

If you or your teens do not have the money to pay with cash, save until you do.

6. Bargain Hunt.

The gas stations to the right of my subdivision price gas three cents a gallon cheaper than the stations to the left in a ritzier area. Where do you think I get fuel? It doesn't sound like much, but over time it adds up. Use the same process in every area of spending and you can save hundreds each year.

Before your teen can make a significant purchase, have him/her price the same item at a minimum of three stores, catalogs, or online stores.

7. Develop Work Ethic.

"Lazy" is a term often associated with teens. Yet, hundreds of fast food restaurants would be out of business without the teen work force. Be on the lookout for teen employers and recommend them to your teen.

If your child is not old enough to get a job, create jobs around the house in addition to the required chores. Don't be cheap; pay teens the same wage per hour they would earn if they did have a job in the "real world." They often learn great work ethics by being rewarded with a check, just like we do.

8. Teach The Dangers Of Greed.

"For the love of money is a root of all kinds of evil. Some people, eager for money, have wandered from the faith and pierced themselves with many grief's" (I Timothy 6:10). Someone stated, "It's OK to have money, but it's not OK for money to have you."

Focus your teen on having a servant spirit. Challenge them to think about what money can do for others, rather than what money can do for self.

9. Seek Advice From Financially Successful Christians.

A non-Christian's point of view may bring riches, but at the expense of character.

Contact a wealthy member of your congregation and invite him/her over for supper and a conversation about financial wisdom. Make sure that you let your guests know that you are going to "pick their brain."

10. Watch The News.

Every night on CNN or a national newscast there is a report about the day's financial gains or loses.

Learning about money isn't always interesting, so cherish the moments you have together watching the ticker tape scroll across the screen.

Dear Parents,

Money is talked about a lot in Scripture, and we have tried to talk about it a lot in our home. Today there are many resources available for teaching kids the X's and O's of money management, and we encourage all parents to take advantage of those. We think the most important thing to teach our kids about money, however, is the concept of stewardship.

First of all, we try to teach to our kids that money is neither good nor evil, for it comes from God. An abundance or lack of money does not make one worldly or righteous. How we use the money God has given us, however, is a reflection of our priorities. We stress that one day we will give an account to God of how we have used the money He has entrusted to us.

Secondly, we teach our kids what the Lord Jesus said, "It is more blessed to give than to receive." We really believe that God has given us money to help others and to further His kingdom. We teach the promises of Scripture that God honors and blesses those who give in faith.

How does this concept of stewardship look in our home? Well, we pray about all financial matters. When we were searching for a new home a few years ago, we prayed in front of each home we were considering. Before entering the mall for a shopping venture, we might pause in the car to pray for God's guidance before we spend His money. We pray as a family for wisdom before making any significant purchase.

Ultimately, our children will probably grow up to view money as we do. They live with us day in and day out, and they can tell if we are more concerned with laying up eternal treasures in heaven or with accumulating temporal treasures here on Earth. As parents, we need to pray that our hearts be right concerning money, lift our kids to God in prayer concerning money, and then turn our kids over to God! Amen!

Serving God,
Al and Candie Crosby

Chapter 14

10 Tips to Help Your Teen Thrive in School

1. Start Each Year Focused.

The older teens become, the more likely their goal is to "just graduate." When the education system is not used to further social and intellectual development, it becomes nothing more than teen-sitting service. Of course, the degree to which your teen thrives in school is related to the desire to do so.

The week before school begins, sit down together and determine the goals for the year. Take a statement as simple as, "By the end of the year I want to _____." Have your teen fill in the blank as many times as needed with specific goals. Such as, "By the end of the year I want to have a "B" average in geometry." Do not be unrealistic with your goals. Make them obtainable, reach them, and set higher ones next time.

2. Maintain A Schedule.

Students are used to following a schedule at school, so do the same at home. Your family may decide that study time is the moment you get home, or it may wait until after supper.

Even school has field trips that change the schedule. Occasionally surprise your child with a field trip of your own.

3. Create A Study Atmosphere.

As you do in your family meetings, cut out any distraction that will encroach on your teen's study habits. Turn off or turn down the phone, television, radio and anything else that could distract.

Ask your teens if there is anything you could provide that would help them study (besides a bribe!). Would a desk area in their room help? Would your availability to help with test questions help?

4. Maintain A Mission Mindset.

Jesus sent His followers out with a mission to go into all the world (Matthew 28:19-20). Send your teen out with the same mission. We need to help teens see that school is a fantastic place to introduce others to Christ.

After a few weeks of school, sit down with your teen and make a list of the classmates he/she knows have not accepted Christ as Savior. Pray together over those names each week and encourage your child to look for opportunities to fulfill the mission.

5. Study Partners.

Are your teens serious enough about their schoolwork to study and not socialize with a partner? If so, then having someone to aid the learning process can be invaluable. It teaches teens to work together for a solution, which is exactly what will be required upon entering the work force.

If you are unsure about your teen's ability to use a study partner for its true intentions, then give it a trial run. Let your teen study with a friend for a couple of tests to see if any improvement results. Have the study area where you can be aware of what is going on.

6. Proper Rest.

Ben Franklin said, "Early to bed and early to rise makes a man healthy, wealthy, and wise." I am not sure about the wealthy part, but I can attest to the healthy and wise aspects. Pure and simply, we cannot function at our physical and mental best without rest.

This may sound old fashioned, but set weeknight bedtimes for the entire family. As your teen matures he/she will feel that age permits staying up later and later. If you set a standard for the family, everyone will be under the same fair guideline.

7. Note How They Take Notes.

Most teachers test from their notes rather than textbooks. If that is true of your child's teacher, ask to review the class notes to determine if your child is a good note taker or not.

Taking good notes is more than being able to copy what is on the overhead or chalkboard. It includes the ability to understand what was written. Teach your teen to write down the notes and anything else that will help to remember the purpose for the notes being given. Teach them to listen for clues such as the teacher saying, "You will see this again."

8. Tackle The Tough Subjects First.

Finishing a study period in failure is discouraging. Have your teen save the easy stuff for last so they can end with a positive feeling.

Tough subjects can be so tough that teens don't want to get started. If that is true for your home, let your teen start with one easy subject, move to the hard one, then close the study session with another easy assignment.

9. Research And Resources.

Today's teens are weaned on a computer and have developed into extreme web surfers, but how many can use a library? Without discounting the importance of the Internet show your teen that other educated resources are available such as periodicals, newspapers, and the news.

If your teen displays interests in learning how to do library research, have them visit your local public or college library. They will be happy to help you learn to use of the library effectively.

10. Personal Responsibilities.

Teens can thrive and survive in school by being held accountable for their own actions towards their grades. Their attitude should be a bad grade is not "the teacher's fault," but "my fault."

When we as parents provide an example of personal responsibility our teens are likely to follow.

Added Bonus: Put up a weekly chart so your teen can see how their study time is affecting their grades. They will find that the more quality time they put into their studies, the better their grades will be and the better they will feel about themselves.

Dear Parents,

Good study habits can make or break your teen's success in school. Knowing how to study and learn assigned materials instead of memorizing facts for the tests is essential. It is imperative that good study habits are developed from the beginning.

Setting up a study area with all necessary supplies is one of the greatest things you can ever do for your teen. By doing this, you are letting them know that you value what they learn and how they excel in school. You are also letting them know that you think their assignments and the way they are prepared are important.

Be a constant encouragement to your teens. Build them up in every way possible. There is a big world waiting for them. If your teens experience success before stepping out into that world they will be way ahead of the game.

Preparing and learning to pass educational hurdles in ones young life will teach them the right way to prepare to pass life's tests later. You, the parent, are the spiritual leader of your teen. Remember, it is your task to bring your teen up in the way he or she should go. Be there for them when times are good and when times are not so good. You should be their greatest supporter!

May God bless you,
Mary Jo and Rodney Shephard

Chapter 15

10 Tips For Helping Your Teen Develop A Positive Self-Image

1. Explain "As You Love Yourself."

With so much talk of humility, most teens think that means to hate yourself. Denying self and hating self are two entirely different things. Explain how God wants teens to "love your neighbor as yourself." Loving self doesn't mean being in love with yourself. It means that we have a good self-image, a God-image. We are important not because of who we are, but *whose* we are.

Whether the world thinks we're geeks or freaks, weirdoes or wackos, only God's view and vision of us counts. And to Him we are worth the price of His Son hammered to a cross.

2. Admit Your Insecurities.

As a parent, you may appear larger than life to teens. They may look at you and think, "I'll never have it together like that." We know the truth. We're not together. We have struggles, bad hair days, and poor complexions at times.

When it's appropriate, share the things that cause your self-esteem to shrink. Share as well the ways that the Lord strengthens you when you don't feel so hot.

3. Encourage Self-Talk.

Tell your teens to stand in front of the mirror every morning and night and repeat, "God don't make no junk," or "I'm made in God's image." It might sound silly, but we really do believe what we say to ourselves.

It may be impossible to get your teen to repeat that phrase out loud because of the risk of being teased. Write a few God-esteem sentences on a 3 x 5 card and give to your child to carry with him or her.

4. Help Teens Challenge Themselves.

Get your teens proactive in the war against insecurity. A

girl might decide that she will stop buying magazines that promote the "perfect look." A guy might choose to stop listening to music that degrades God's creation by elevating suicide over life.

In place of those negatives, your daughter may want to start reading a Christian magazine for young ladies, while your son might toss out his CD collection and replace it with Christian artists. We are what we absorb, so challenge your teens to challenge themselves.

5. Provide Ways For Teens To Give Of Themselves.

It's tough to feel sorry for yourself when your eyes are on others. Paul tells us in Philippians 2:4 that we should look not only on our interests, but also the interests of others.

Keep a list of area organizations that use teens for volunteers. When your child comes home looking low and using terms that beat up his emotions, send him down to the area children's hospital and let him share his life.

6. Support Teen Accountability Groups.

Encourage your teens to share their insecurities with the peers they trust. All of us have a low self-esteem about something. Teens will find comfort in knowing that everyone has weaknesses and that they are not alone.

It's critical that these groups be made up of individuals who respect one another. One "cool dude" could blow the whole effort with his insensitivity.

7. Provide Articles That Relate To Their Struggle.

Most of us can handle a problem more effectively if we understand the problem. If you run across an article called "Beauty is Only Skin Deep" that talks about godliness being more important than looks, cut it out and place it on your teen's dresser. If you have some who feel untalented, or unneeded, clip out some articles that talk about Moses being God's chosen, but reluctant, servant.

Be cautious when sharing these articles. Those receiving them could think you agree with their plight. The girl who feels unattractive might think, "Mom obviously thinks I'm ugly or she wouldn't have sent this story."

8. Help Teens Remain Focused.

Teens may become apathetic or lazy when consumed by a low self-esteem. Help them take their mind off themselves by helping them stay focused.

Keep a mental list of important events in your teen's life and ask about them.

9. "Patience, Grasshopper."

The teacher on "Kung Fu" always reminded his student to remain patient. No one can master Kung Fu overnight, it takes years. Teens won't master their self-esteem over night either. Tell them to remain patient and to allow the Master to shape them in His time.

Study I Peter 5:6 together.

10. Help Teens Identify The Problem And Be Proactive.

Some problems are more mental than physical. Help teens discover the root of the problem and provide a way to overcome it.

Make sure the root of the issue is discovered. It may be that attractiveness is not the real cause of the hurt. Acceptance may be the real problem.

Dear Parents,

God has blessed us with three very different children, currently ages 22, 19, and 12. Each one is unique in so many ways that we have often wondered if they truly came from the same gene pool. If you have two or more children, you have, no doubt, asked the same question, "Are these really ours?" In spite of the varied personalities, talents and needs, as parents we want the same thing for each of our children—contentment on Earth and an eternity with God. Finding ways to assure their positive self-image will naturally lead to contentment.

We asked our daughters and a close friend of theirs what parents can do to help with the development of their self-image. I asked them to "look back" and share what we might have done that was right. Several responses were good:

(1) When your child is young, "set-up" successes for them. Ours didn't realize what was happening at the time, but now they realize that we knew they would succeed at a challenge we helped plan. It was challenging for them, yet attainable.

(2) Avoid over-advising as the child grows. Loosening up goes hand-in-hand with the maturing of the child. Trust God to guide and direct them and their self-esteem will continue to grow with every right decision they make.

(3) We spent, and still spend, a lot of time in conversation with our children. It is very important to let them be heard and to be made to feel like what they are saying is very important to us as parents. There are many times when we would like to interrupt and explain a better way it was hard, but we were silent.

(4) One of the greatest self-image builders is for our children to know that they are loved and appreciated. They need to know that we understand that they will make mistakes. They also need to know that we will help them work through those mistakes.

(5) The last thing seems so simple, but yet it is so important. We pray and turn our concerns over to God. We ask Him to be with our children as they face different areas of life. We pray for Him to develop the kind of self-image which will give glory to Him and not to the child.

Serving Him,
Mark & Jacque Loudermilk

Chapter 16

10 Family Traditions To Build On

1. Christmas.

This holiday is one of the fondest traditions of all times. Families draw closer together during this holiday of giving and receiving.

Don't wait until December to start planning your traditions. Get your calendar out by June and mark important Christmas dates such as caroling, baking goodies for those without families, etc.

2. Birthdays.

As we grow older we often want others to forget our birthdays and the number of years associated with them. But to a teen, birthdays are significant because each one brings with it more freedom and more responsibility.

Switch from a birthday to a birth week! Make a list of seven significant people in your teens lives. Ask each one to write a special note telling why the young person is special to him or her. Give one note a day to your teens during the week preceding their birthday.

3. Den Camping.

This is a great idea and works wonders with young teens and pre-teens. Grab a mattress, sleeping bags, and pillows and camp out in your living room.

Turn off anything electrical that might interfere with your time together. Use gas lamps or candles. Play board games or talk. Rise early the next morning and make pancakes as a family.

4. Memory Night.

Pull out the scrapbooks and photo albums and relive the moments your family has spent together. Teens will love to see the polyester outfits you used to wear. And all will enjoy being reminded of tender and terrific family times.

Share something with your kids about your teen years. Think of a special memory with your family, or an embarrassing act. Better yet, tell about a time when your parents embarrassed you, then your teens will realize it runs as just part of the parental family tree.

5. Helping Hands.

Take on a benevolent project as a family. Ask about the ongoing service areas at your church to see if there is a place to get plugged in. If not, call your Chamber of Commerce and ask about area soup kitchens, or service organizations.

Get together with your teen and study Luke 3:11; Mark 10:45; Acts 6:1; Galatians 2:10; James 2:15. These verses will help your family understand the importance of being "helping hands."

6. Anniversaries.

If you are married celebrate your anniversary in a visible way. Let your teen see the love you have for each other. Hug and kiss in an appropriate way in front of your family so your teen can have a mental image of godly affection.

Make a tradition of a variety of anniversaries. Honor the memory of a passed family member by placing flowers on the grave once a year. When an employment milestone is reached use it to teach your teen about longevity in the workplace.

7. Mother's Day/Father's Day.

These are two days that even teens know they are supposed to remember. They don't know exactly what to do with it, but they know something positive is expected.

Help your teen plan for the day. If you are a dad, give advice about making Mother's Day special. If you are a mom, help your kids move beyond the basic tie gift into a realm of actual thought and consideration.

8. Family Reunions.

For teens a family reunion is about as much fun as acne. Unknown faces pinch their cheeks and talk about how much they have grown since the last time everyone was together. Clue your teen in on the reasons for the time together and what it can mean to your family.

Before the reunion get out the family photos and provide a family tree refresher course so no one at the party will seem like a stranger.

9. Thanksgiving.

Turkey, dressing, and pumpkin pie adorn many tables on the fourth Thursday of November. Use the time as more than just a reason to feast Fast for at least fifteen minutes before carving the bird to give each person present an opportunity to express their thanks for the people in the room.

To help prod conversation, begin each blessing with a simple phrase such as, "I'm thankful for..." With everyone beginning with those same words no one should feel that another's thanks was better.

10. Family Vacations.

National Lampoon's series of vacation movies starring Chevy Chase are enough to keep any family off the road and out of the air. How many disaster family vacations have you been on or read about? Yet, when we decide not to take time off together we miss some of the richest moments in life.

Agree unanimously on the vacation of choice. If anyone is told, "We are going to Canada, and you will have a good time!" a bad time is guaranteed.

Dear Parents,

Traditions are those special things that are passed down from generation to generation. Most of the traditions that our family has are focused on times that we spend together.

One of the simple traditions we have is eating our evening meal together. Ever since the kids were young, even though Junior worked late at times, we usually ate our evening meal together. It's a time at the end of the day when everybody can tell about their day and just be together. We also started at this time the tradition of holding hands when praying before the meals. It started out that we were trying to keep the children's hands out of things but has become a symbol of a bond we have together. Take advantage of these times as long as you can because the older the kids get the harder it is to juggle schedules to have just these simple times together.

For birthdays we usually go out to eat at the person that's having the birthday's favorite restaurant. We used to have a big party for the kids together and invite the whole family on both sides and have a big cookout. It was a fun time and I think it helped them realize that their family loved them.

Another thing we do is try to spend at least one week together in the summer for a vacation. It could be a trip to the beach, a trip to the mountains, and, when our daughter graduated from high school, we went on a cruise. We always have special memories of these trips that we still talk about.

Another tradition we have is having a short devotional or prayer before we go to bed at night. This assures the children that they are always in our prayers. That is the most important thing you can ever do for them.

We also get together at different times of the year with other members of our family. Mainly at Thanksgiving, Christmas and other various times during the year.

An important thing to us is to include your teens when you're doing things for others. Whether it be going to see visitors who have come to church, cut grass, go see shut-ins, taking food, etc. Your children learn from seeing you do things like this for others.

Always pray with them and for them every day. Give them back to God and give Him the glory and you will be richly blessed.

Serving Him,
James and Becky Bagwell

Chapter 17

10 Responsibilities Of A Christian Father

1. Be The Spiritual Leader.

Households today are filled with men who do little to lead their families toward Jesus. They feel their responsibility is to provide income, but not spiritual guidance for their home.

Lead by modeling your life after Jesus. Paul said, "Imitate me as I imitate Christ." You should be able to say the same to your family. In what ways are you presently modeling the image of Jesus? What are two areas you could improve?

2. Meet Your Family's Mental, Physical, And Spiritual Needs.

Each person under your roof has a specific set of needs that must be touched in order for him or her to become what God desires.

Meet mental needs by asking about the feelings and emotions of the day. Meet physical needs by supporting athletic endeavors in a balanced way. Meet spiritual needs by always being the first to mention prayer, devotional, or worship.

3. Discipline With Love.

Every kid has heard, "I'm doing this because I love you." I discovered the truth behind that statement about eight years after high school (when I had my first child!). Love, not anger, is the proper way to shape a life. As a man you may find it challenging not to discipline with a hard hand. Choose to discipline with a soft heart.

Discipline is not always negative. Because of our tendency to come across in a gruff manner, it is critical for men to show the positive aspects of their punishment method. Explain precisely to your teen the reason behind your discipline.

4. Affirm Your Teenager.

"Do not let any unwholesome talk come out of your mouths, but only what is helpful for building others up according to their needs," Ephesians 4:29. It's natural for dads to be tough instead of tender. Think about the personality of your teen. What words does he/she need to hear from you?

Someone quipped, "If you want to get rid of a minister just pat him on the back. He will work himself to death because of your encouragement." Affirmation produces the fruit of expectation among teenagers. They begin to become what you encourage.

5. Motivate.

Coaches know how to get their teams geared up for a game. They use a combination of words, training, and direction to move their players to the desired action. Fire up your teen for life by continually providing positive words, training and direction for him/her.

Read books by Zig Ziglar or John Maxwell to get a clear picture of motivation. Their resources will help you achieve a higher standard for life, and provide the tools needed to help your teen do the same.

6. Build on Family Experiences.

TBS regularly shows the movie, *The Good, the Bad, and the Ugly*. That same title could describe many of our family experiences. All three areas contribute valuable lessons for life. For example, when your teenage daughter's face breaks out just before her date (the bad and ugly combined), use it as an opportunity to talk to her about inner beauty.

Reach into your memory bank to discover how experiences with your father or grandfather shaped your life. Consider how you can use those memories to enhance your and your child's relationship.

7. Don't Waste a Minute.

A few years ago a survey revealed that the average father thought he talked twenty to thirty minutes a day with his

84

child. Actual test subjects revealed that an average of 15 seconds was used each day in conversation.

Forget the lie of quality time verses quantity time. Without quantity there can be no quality. A dad never surveyed his life from his deathbed and said, "I spent too much time with my family."

8. Model Great Dads.

Who comes to mind when you think of an awesome dad? What makes him great? What characteristics do you notice that you have in your life that resembles that person? What qualities are lacking?

Call the great dad you have in mind and take him out to lunch. Have a list of questions prepared so you can learn from the individual.

9. Make Home Your Top Priority.

If a stranger were to ask your wife and children about the most important thing in your life, what would the answer be? Would God be first? Would family be second? If not, sit down right now and work out the details necessary to reorganize the priorities of your life.

Let your family hold you accountable. When you promise to be home by 6 p.m., but you don't get home until 7 p.m., have a penalty set. Maybe you have to take the family out to eat. A few missed deadlines will hurt your heart and your wallet.

10. Demonstrate the Love of Christ.

Many men I know knew the heavy hand of their fathers growing up, but not their love. Show your love to your family.

Is there any unresolved problem with your teen at this time? If so, offer forgiveness with no strings attached.

Dear Parents,

As the father of four grown children, I have just recently given myself totally to the Lord. He is in control of everything that I do. How I wish I had done that when my children were growing up. Yes, we took them to the services of the Church, and yes we taught them to be good moral people. I know now that we never taught them to love the Lord, just to obey Him, and there is a difference. I was a good disciplinarian and they respected us. However, I wish that my children could have heard me pray more often, I wish that they could have seen me with my open Bible more often. I was a good father but I wasn't a good example. Although they knew that I loved them very much, it was difficult for me to demonstrate God's love. I have learned to move self to the back and others to the front and to be a servant. If I could leave you with but one thought it would be to show your love for others, and in so doing you will show your love for God. We both know that we made so many mistakes, but there is no going back. Children learn so much by example. May God bless you as you raise your children.

Sincerely,
Carl Hopson

Chapter 18

10 Tips For Recognizing
Teen Depression

1. Appearance.

In some teens, depression will produce ongoing sorrow with a look of ongoing hopelessness. Their skin tone can lose its healthy color. Some appear frail and weakened by their depression.

Ask about their lives. Their appearance could be attributed to a relationship breakup, or another cause.

2. Eating Disorders.

Overeating, anorexia, and bulimia can all result from depression. They are all coping mechanisms.

If a teen is acting abnormally down or continually complains about his or her body, casually watch their eating patterns. Do they gorge? Do they always rush to the restroom after a meal?

3. Insomnia.

This is not lack of sleep, but the inability to sleep. A teen's melancholy may keep him awake. He wants to sleep, he needs his rest, but it won't come.

When your teen talks about not being able to sleep ask about how long it has gone on. If it's just a couple of nights, ask again in a few days. If it's been months, investigate further.

4. Lack Of Concentration.

Do any teens drift into their own world? Do you notice their inability to focus regardless of the situation? Depression can take you miles away from reality. Everything is filtered through the lens of doubt and insecurity. The tendency is for the lack of focus to show up as apathy. You may notice your teens displaying an "I don't care" attitude more than usual.

Give a specific task for your teen to focus on for a short period of time. This should help him/her increase their ability to concentrate.

5. Suicidal Thoughts.

Severe cases of depression bring on thoughts of taking one's life. One feels as if there is nothing to live for. Nothing holds significance under the fog of depression. Because of the intense hopelessness, teens may think their families, friends, or the world as a whole would be better off without them. They may think that since their emotional downs affect them so greatly they must have the same effects on others.

Research the web, medical books, or ask your family doctor for information on suicidal tendencies.

6. No Vision.

Talk to teens struggling with this problem and they will tell you about a bleak future with no light at the end of the tunnel. They have no vision for their lives. They believe others can and will succeed, but their lives are doomed to sub-mediocrity.

Don't go overboard with this, but do reveal some aspects of their lives that hold promise. They may not believe you at the time, but when they are in an up mode they will remember your encouragement.

7. Extreme Weight Loss.

While some teens over eat when they are depressed, others choose to under eat. They may blame their weight for the feelings they have and choose to "diet" to change their appearance and thus change their mood. They don't realize that a large portion of their negative self-image has been created by their negative mental state.

Keep a soft eye on the scales. Do not misjudge your teen's weight gain or loss. Be more conscious about the rate at which weight changes, not the amount.

8. No Energy.

I spoke with a young lady last week who said, "I don't want to get out of bed. I don't want to go to school or the mall. I don't even want to turn the lights on, I just want to sleep." Some depressed teens feel tired all the time. Caffeine or calories make no difference. All they want to do is sleep, which, of course, allows them to escape their struggle.

Busy moms and dads can miss glaring signs of a problem and are quick to accept a teen's excuse. Don't be so busy that you miss obvious signs of your child's declining health.

9. Strong Feelings Of Guilt.

Depression magnifies negative feelings of anger, sorrow, and guilt. It can cause a teen to remember a sin from several years ago and renew the guilt as if it just occurred.

Remind teens that forgiveness is forever. We have God's promise that He will always forgive us no matter the depth of the sin (I John 1:9).

10. Overly Sensitive.

This is a no brainer. Kids that used to be able to dish it out and take it as well are no longer able to endure the casual teasing. They take it personally and use it to feed the insecurity brought on by their depression.

Be sensitive to the sensitive and pass the same advice on to the rest of the family. An easy target gets more of the rough comments than a person who doesn't care. Be protective when your teen is showing characteristics of depression.

Dear Parents,

It is difficult to write words of encouragement about depression. We initially ignored the warning signs of our son's illness, because we believed it was a behavioral problem. Addressing clinical depression as a simple behavioral problem compounds the problem rather than resolving it. We finally did something to address the problem of our son's depression, but the psychologist who initially treated him diagnosed a learning disability as the cause of his problems. Following years of mis-diagnosis and deepening psychological problems, our son was finally diagnosed correctly. He now takes medication and visits a therapist on a regular basis. His situation is much improved, and our ability to accept his problems for what they are has also improved.

Some parents ignore the warning signs of depression and hope the illness will resolve itself without treatment. We encourage you not to let your child's depression go untreated. Ignoring it can lead to other, more serious problems. There are many new medications and a variety of therapies available to treat depression. Early diagnosis and treatment are the keys to achieving a livable situation with your child. Christian counseling and prayer help the child and the family achieve a sense of wellness.

A personal relationship with Jesus Christ is essential to your child's recovery from depression. Our son has told us many times he was able to get through his darkest hours by relying on prayer and his favorite passages from the Bible. Family prayer time with our son helped all of us to understand each other and pull together as a family in times of crisis.

Sincerely,
Ken and Linda Dunham

Chapter 19

10 Spiritual Checkpoints For Parents

1. Daily Quiet Time With God.

Relationships bloom when couples spend time together. Are you and God a couple? If so, it will be reflected by the time you share with each other.

Set a specific time each day to get together with God. It may sound coarse to place the Lord in our schedules, but many of us will neglect Him if we don't. Over time the regular time set aside for Him will become automatic.

2. Bible Study.

Bible study may or may not be part of your daily time with God. If it is be sure to center the time on study rather than reading. Rick Warren, pastor of Saddleback Community Church, states "the difference between reading and study is that you use a pen when you study."

Like a quiet time, Bible study needs to be daily. Acts 17:11 says that the Bereans, "...examined the Scriptures every day..."

3. Purposed Giving.

"But just as you excel in everything—in faith, in speech, in knowledge, in complete earnestness and in your love for us—see that you also excel in this grace of giving" – 2 Corinthians 8:7. Think about financial resources as God's resources. We are spending God's money. We are investing God's treasures.

4. Church Attendance.

Granted, showing up for church services does not guarantee spiritual maturity. Not attending, however, speaks about our life's priorities and our children witness those priorities. Hebrews 10:26 make it clear that we come together on Sunday to give and receive encouragement. Christian fellowship is an added bonus for us to enjoy.

Use the ride home after worship to talk about the ways you were encouraged. Share positive comments you received or talk about the impact of the sermon on your life.

5. Helping Others.

It has been said that we often have difficulty between service and serve us. The life of Jesus reveals to us a life of service (Mark 10:45). The Apostle Paul later echoed this lifestyle by indicating that a servant spirit reflects the life of Christ (Philippians 2:1-11).

Think about the ways you have served others in the past, and how others have reached out to you. List three ways you have served others in the past month. And write down three ways you will serve in the coming month.

6. Witnessing.

"Go into all the world..." Jesus begins in the great commission. Our world starts with our friends, family, and neighbors.

Pray right now for God to place someone in your life today that you can talk to about His Son. Also, pray that God with give you words of wisdom as you share.

7. Faith Development.

As our bodies age, so does our faith. Hopefully, it becomes more mature and dependable. By the end of our days our trust and dependence on God should have grown significantly since the early days of our faith.

Read Hebrews 11 and make a list of all the people mentioned in this chapter of faith. Choose one that you feel you relate to the most and ask God to give you the same faith as the person you selected.

8. Fellowship With Other Believers.

We become like our focus. Surrounding ourselves with a variety of Christians will strengthen our faith and form holy friendships. The early church spent a lot of time developing this facet (Acts 2:42-47).

Once a month invite a family into your home for a meal or just to visit.

9. Contacting And Caring.

The "we missed you" factor is overlooked in many churches. When we contact those who miss worship, class, or small group they learn that we care.

Keep a list of those in your class and small group. Anytime someone is absent, send a note or make a phone call just to let them know how much you missed them.

10. Speak Positively Of Others.

Dale Carnegie said that we should treat people like we mine gold. You have to move a lot of dirt to find the gold, but you're not looking for dirt, you're looking for gold.

Ignore the dirt and look for the gold in others. When you spot a special nugget draw attention to it through conversation by pointing out the positive attribute in the person.

Dear Parents,

Once at a parenting seminar, the presenter shared this insightful truth, likening raising children to playing baseball. In the game, the parents are the catcher and umpire, always standing behind home plate, while the children play the outfield. Being children, they frequently crowd the out of bounds fence and sometimes even jump it chasing balls. This presents the temptation for parents to begin moving away from home plate, edging towards the children. With the catcher and umpire no longer behind home plate, the rules of the game begin to change. Her wise counsel to parents was to never ever leave home plate, so that the children will always know where to find you. One's faith in Jesus Christ, coupled with a clear sense of right and wrong must remain the immovable home plate on which the game of life is played.

Joe and I felt that this "home plate" concept was one factor in the lives of our two teenagers that we had some control over. We saw many of our friends follow their children from congregation to congregation, depending on where their friends were going or which youth program was the most popular at the time. We also were saddened to see so many marriages shaken, as the parents could not agree on how certain teen issues should be handled with their own family. We also witnessed some parents who quit coming to church altogether because they were so embarrassed by their teens' behavior. Observing these things, we worked hard at presenting a united front when dealing with issues. We wanted our teens to see that their parents were committed to each other and to the Lord, when they were seeing so many families dissolve. We hoped that our example of faith would be one that would make an impression as they found themselves in new situations day after day. We wanted them to have a sense of security knowing exactly where we stood on home plate!

One of the most helpful things we did during this time of life was to seek out other families we respected who had survived the teen years and who could give us advice as parents and as a Christian couple, much as you are doing as you read this book. We also planned at least one summer time "spiritual growth" seminar where our family could go for strength, reassurance and reaffirmation of our faith. Anytime we were traveling, we listened to tapes by Christian "professionals" who encouraged personal growth and to Christian music for our praise to God. Encouraging scriptures such as "I can do all things through Christ who strengthens me" and "All things work together for good to those who love the Lord and are called according to His purpose" and "Bring up a child in the way he should go, and when he is old, he will not depart from it" played a very important part of our daily lives, as well as the basic faith builders of prayer and staying in God's Word. We continually encouraged each other by keeping communication lines open and building each other up, strengthening our marriage relationship. Teen years can be very trying times... rewarding and, unfortunately, at times discouraging.

We don't know yet the outcome of our staying on home plate as far as our children are concerned. We really don't know what the future holds, but we do know who holds the future.

In Him,
Joe and Jane Keller

Chapter 20

10 Tips For Dealing With Power Struggles

1. Consistency.

When it comes to behavior we like predictability. A person who blows up one time, then acts calm the next time the same event occurs makes us nervous. Our children will try to wrestle control when they see that we display little ability to react in the same manner in identical situations.

Write a paragraph detailing consistent and inconsistent areas of your life that your teen could pick up on. Pinpoint the circumstance you show the least consistency.

2. Walk Away.

Watch any professional sport and you will witness officials and players arguing at some period of the game. If the player refuses to back off, he or she risks being tossed out of the game. Ultimately, we have the power of restriction or discipline when it comes to our children, but like the sports official, we are not often liked after the struggle.

Determine a walk-away level when a confrontation rises above a certain level. It may be raising the voice, getting personal, etc. Return to the conversation when the atmosphere is workable. Explain it is time to end the discussion to and pick it up later after a period of "cooling off."

3. Never Argue In Public.

Have you ever witnessed a family blowup in the mall? All parties involved look ridiculous. Save the corrections and explanations until you get home, or at least to the car.

If the struggle cannot wait until you get back to the house move to a place out of the sight of onlookers, and out of earshot. A storeowner would prefer your conflict take place in their back office than on the department floor.

4. Establish A Procedure.

Before every flight the attendants go over the same detailed rules "in case of an emergency." Put together a plan for your family to follow in the case of a power struggle emergency. If your family tends to explode, your first step may be taking a twenty minute time out. If your family is less emotional, you may want to begin by listing the reasons for your position.

Establish the rules collectively. The procedure you choose should benefit all family members so everyone has the same advantage.

5. Communicate The Consequences.

Set a clear and concise punishment that will coincide with a power struggle. As mentioned earlier in the book, setting a specific standard will enable you to carry out the consequences without argument. A rule that has been made is difficult to fight against.

Have all family members agree to and sign your "power struggle covenant" so it will be known that everyone understands the standard.

6. Deal With Current Issues.

Reopening old wounds brings with it the risk of infection. Keep your family clean by sticking with issues that affect your family in the present.

Make a verbal pact with your teenager that you will not hold past struggles against him or her. Set up a consequence for yourself that your teen may hold you responsible for if you fail to remain true (maybe treat them to a movie).

7. Avoid Anger.

As parents we all lose it occasionally and discipline our children out of anger rather than love. Nowhere is the temptation greater than during a power struggle. We feel our control being wrestled away and our pride steps in and takes over.

Memorize James 1:19-20, "My dear brothers and sisters, be quick to listen, slow to speak, and slow to get angry. Your anger can never make things right in God's sight" (NLT).

8. Admit When You Are Wrong.

When the President of the United States takes advantage of his position for personal purposes it's called abuse of power. Our parental position places the same risk on us. "Because I said so," is the number one answer when we as parents have few answers.

Most of us are blind to our missteps. Once a month sit down with your teen and ask him or her where you have taken advantage of your parental power. If your teen makes a good point, apologize and grow from the experience.

9. Plan Ahead.

We listen to the weather before taking a trip to the beach or lake. We consult a map before venturing cross-country (hopefully). Likewise, we should consider the difficulties in the road ahead before we come to them. How will we handle teen pregnancy, academic challenges, or sneaking out of the house at night?

Call on several of your church or community families who have children in their twenties. Ask them about the struggles they faced when their kids were teens and use the information to prepare you for the possibilities.

10. Stay Focused.

God seeks godly offspring (Malachi 2:15).

Each morning thank God for your teens and pray for your gentleness and their openness when it comes to the power of your home.

Dear Parents,

Don't feel like you are alone; most parents deal with power struggles with their teens. Some parents have to tackle this more often than they would like. Sometimes, the issue is trivial to one side and a matter of life and death to the other side. Yes, these sides are interchangeable. It's a tightrope to be walked. Our children are at an age where we want them to be making more of their own decisions, accepting responsibility for their actions and deeds and yet it is still our responsibility to question their decisions. Sometimes it is our responsibility to make a better decision.

Part of the power struggle is more than getting your child to think through the situation. Yes, we want them to sort through the pros and cons, the good and the bad, when making a decision. We also want them to learn self-control. Accepting the "no's" is something with which we all struggle. After all, it's not just parents who say no. Do you take "no" well? Can your child learn self-control by watching you?

Our children make mistakes; so do we. We ask our children to admit their wrongs. We should be able to admit ours. Graciously and with full honesty, just like we ask them to. Admitting an error can go a long way in strengthening your relationship with your child.

If you feel that your efforts in conquering power struggles are failing, you are not alone. We all have our regrets about decisions made in the heat of the moment, or when we were on an emotional overload. This is a time when you hit your knees and tell your heavenly Father you can't handle this alone. Of course, He knows this, but it's good for us to admit our failings.

We can no more be perfect parents than we can be perfect spouses; perfect employees or, a few years back, perfect children. We can only do the best we can; the Lord will take care of the rest.

Sincerely,
Butch & Roanne Norris

Chapter 21

10 Tips For Developing Your Teen's Talents

1. Fully Support Their Talent(s).

Pursue your teen's talent with him or her by making yourself accessible for pick-ups and drop-offs when needed. Give praise when it is warranted. Talk about how proud you are without expanding their egos.

It is possible for a parent to try to press a teen into a certain mold. A particular sport may be your talent, but not your teen's. A certain instrument may have brought you acclaim, but your teen may dislike the instrument. Support your teen's talent, not your talent through your teen.

2. Provide Guidance For Their Choices.

Part of our roles as parents is to protect our children from preventable hurt. Without being too critical on each end of the spectrum, we need to be honest about our child's ability and gently direct him or her.

Help your teen develop specific goals for their gift. Does he or she want to pursue a talent to the hobby, amateur, or professional level? Whatever is chosen, help your child research what it would take to attain the goal.

3. Supply Their Needs For Talent Development.

In addition to equipment costs, help your teen learn about their talent from another perspective. Buy books or tapes that would help them attain their dreams.

Contact someone in your area that is known for his or her ability in the area of your child's talent. Invite him or her over for supper to talk about their talent so your teen can hear about what it takes to reach excellence.

4. Help Them See More Than One Talent.

A teen may recognize that he/she had a great sports ability, but may fail to see the public speaking ability possessed as well.

Create a talent pad. When you notice your child show adeptness in a certain area, write it down on the pad. Every few months share your findings and point out the talents to your teen that he or she may not have been aware of.

5. Consistently Encourage.

"But your assistant, Joshua son of Nun, will enter it. Encourage him, because he will lead Israel to inherit it" (Deuteronomy 1:38). Moses was told that Joshua, not he, would lead Israel into the Promised Land. Joshua had a talent for leadership, but he needed encouragement to keep him going.

Build up without giving the big head. Use notes, hugs, and praise to let your child know how proud you are of him/her.

6. Allow Them To Progress At Their Own Rate.

Many of today's pro athletes were not high school stars. Their talent developed in their college years. What would have happened if they had been pushed too soon? They probably would have burned out and quit their sport.

Don't get caught up in the trap of letting what other people think when it comes to your teens talent. Some parents make their kids sound like the next superstar. Save your teens the embarrassment by allowing them to grow at their own rate.

7. Apply Positive Peer Pressure.

Allowing teens to progress at their speed does not mean you cannot encourage them to expand their abilities. It's difficult for any parent to sit back and watch their child waste his potential.

Have a dream night and allow your teens to express what they would be if they could take their talent to its greatest length. After you have their expressions use them as reminders when slackness shows up in the pursuit of the dream.

8. Never Compare Them With Other Teens.

It seems that comparison with a peer would prod a teen

to greater goals. Usually they either get discouraged by their lack of skill, or they get arrogant in their superiority.

Speak in terms of "could be" rather than "should be." "Should be" communicates where you believe a teen ought to be presently. "Could be" encourages a teen to reach a point some time in the future.

9. Encourage Them Not To Give Up Too Soon.

There may come a time when it's obvious that a teen will not reach the pinnacle desired. Other times a teen gives in before putting the time and effort into a talent to reap the benefits.

When a teen fills your ears with "I'm just not good enough," or "I'll never make it", keep encouraging him/her to keep working and give it all their best effort until it's clear that this particular talent should not be their goal.

10. Teach Them To Be Thankful For Their Talents.

The Bible encourages us to give thanks for everything. God is the one who placed the gifts and abilities in us, so it is only appropriate to give Him the glory for our skills.

During a family devotional sing "Thank You, Lord" or "Give Thanks." Read Exodus 36:1-5 and discuss how God provides abilities for His people.

Dear Parents,

It is so important for parents to help teens develop their talents. We encouraged our children to participate in all activities at school and at church. Our motto was "At least try it!" Our children entered sports activities, speaking contests, talent contests, bike activities, and many Lads to Leaders activities. Our daughter entered baking contests, sewing contests, and other activities in 4-H.

We let our teens make up their minds about participation after some serious discussions with them. If after a certain period of time, they wanted to quit, that was acceptable. We rather insisted that they play sports for a whole year. If after the year, they wanted to drop out, that was fine. We didn't let our children start something and then quit the next day. We felt that they needed some time to make a good decision.

Our children usually decided if they wanted to participate in a contest, but once they had decided we insisted that they follow through. They would say their speeches every day for several weeks to one of us when they were participating in a speaking contest. We were there to encourage and help them. We tried not to be overly critical, but just to offer suggestions. When parents are encouraging children, it is important to keep the communication lines open. Always compliment the teen before offering a suggestion or giving a criticism. They need plenty of praise when things aren't going so well.

We tried to offer transportation for activities, we bought materials for their activities, but probably the most important thing that we did was to be by their side when they were searching for their talents. Besides being at their activities, we were with them at home researching, helping, offering suggestions, making costumes and watching them experiment.

Each child is different, so it is important not to compare one with the other. We had one child who won almost every contest he entered and the other who didn't win. We put emphasis on participating, and each was rewarded for taking part. Today, our daughter will tell you that she benefited from losing contests. We never compared our two children because each is special in their own way.

When our son was making speeches before churches we took him to hear some great preachers. He was very impressed, and this was an added incentive to be better.

It is important to teach our teens to be thankful. We would point out to our teens others who couldn't run or speak and how thankful we should be for our talents. We believe that it is important to stress how special each person is because he has been made by God and has talents that maybe others do not have. We did stress this to our teens.

It is an awesome task to be a parent, and one of our responsibilities is to help our teens develop their talents to their full potential.

In Him,
Jim and Sue Crabtree

Chapter 22

10 Tips For Overcoming Parental Worries

1. Concentrate On Your Blessings, Not Your Worries.

The more attention we give our worries the more consumed we become with them. We find that our troubles fill our minds through all hours of the day, while no solution seems feasible.

Sit down with a legal pad and draw a line down the middle to make two columns. Label the left column "blessings" and the right column "worries." Write down as many as you can in both columns. Don't your blessings easily outnumber your worries? Focus on the blessings from God and allow Him to take care of the rest (Matthew 6:25-34).

2. Design A Plan Of Action For Each Worry.

When most of us worry we think about how awful the situation is or could become, but rarely do we take action to solve the problem. As a general rule, cross any worry off the list that you have no control over and cannot influence through action.

Take the list of worries you made in tip #1 and write a brief action you can take to the side of each one. For example: "I worry about my child's friends." Action: "I will get to know each friend personally."

3. Read Scriptures That Inspire You.

What is your favorite Bible verse? What passage can you turn to at almost any moment and receive encouragement? God gave us His Word not only to reveal Himself, but also to provide hope, joy and peace for day-to-day struggles.

Memorize Philippians 4:6-8 and live by the promises given in these verses.

4. Share Your Worries With Others.

Galatians 6:2 teaches us to bear one another's burdens. The challenge to that verse is that we don't want to share our burdens because we are afraid we will become a burden to others.

Any parent with teens is probably discovering the same worries as you. Invite several parents to your home for a meal and sharing. Use the time to find solutions, not just to share struggles.

5. Inform Yourself About The Health Problems Related To Worry.

High blood pressure, lack of sleep, lack of concentration, and loss of appetite often accompany worry. Any one or a combination of those can cause your mental and physical health to deplete rapidly. Call your physician for complete information on the ill effects of worry.

Monitor your eating and sleeping habits to see if they are affected by worry. Do you notice any changes on the days you are consumed by problems? Do you lie awake wondering what to do? If so, make an appointment with your doctor and discuss your symptoms.

6. Use Mental Exercises.

Worry takes place in the mind. We take our circumstances and build on a set of "What if this happens..." Instead of filling your mind with all the negative things that can occur, fill it with all of the positive things that could occur.

Use books to fill your mind with understanding. Consider reading *How to Stop Worrying and Start Living* by Dale Carnegie; *Don't Worry, Be Happy* by Martin Solomon; or *When You Worry About the Child You Love* by Edward Hallowell.

7. Use Physical Exercise.

Begin your physical regimen with a physical from your doctor. I agree, an examination is not pleasant but it will give your doctor a gauge to go by before starting your program.

Exercise a minimum of thirty minutes three times a

week. Walking, swimming, aerobics, biking, weight training, etc., can all help prevent worry by increasing your physical and mental health.

8. Keep A Prayer Journal.

A prayer journal allows you to keep up with your prayers to God and when and how He answers them. A notebook will do or you can opt for a hardcover book designed specifically for journaling.

Place a "W" beside your prayer requests that involve worry. As God answers the prayer, cross it out to show that God has taken the worry away.

9. Live One Day At A Time.

Jesus said that each day has enough problems of its own, so there is no need to get consumed about the next day (Matthew 6: 34). We have to plan ahead for the future, but there is no need to worry about the future.

Live with eternity in mind. About each event ask yourself, "What is the eternal consequence of this?" Few, if any, of our worries involve eternity; most of them relate to the present world.

10. Throw Your Worries To God.

Say the following out loud, "Cast all your cares on Him, because He cares for you" (I Peter 5:7).

Write each of your worries on a separate slip of paper. Sit in a chair in front of your garbage can. One by one, wad up your worry and pray about it, saying, "God, I am throwing this care away. I trust you to handle it." Then throw the worry in the garbage and forget it.

Dear Parents,

Worrying is a malady which plagues almost every parent, especially those with adolescent children. Since adolescence is a crucial period when lifetime values are developed, it is imperative that parents influence their children in an aggressively positive way. While worry is a natural response to our concerns in the rearing of children, it proves of little value in the developmental process.

As Christian parents, you have available the greatest source of strength and encouragement in your desire for excellence for your children—the power and the efficacy of prayer. The apostle Paul in his letter to the Philippians gave this instruction: "Do not be anxious (do not worry) about anything but in everything, by prayer and petition, with thanksgiving, present your requests to God." Peter puts it this way: "Humble yourselves, therefore, under God's mighty hand, that He may lift you up in due time. Cast all your anxiety on Him because he cares for you."

It all boils down to a matter of one's faith in the Lord. Do you believe that God hears you, cares for you, and will grant your requests if you go to Him in faith? Scripture teaches us that He does!

Isn't it reassuring to know that you're not alone in directing your children? God's mighty hand is there to assist you! What else could you ever desire or need? Just call upon Him, trust in Him and then claim His promise.

Thankful,
Dick and Dorris Thompson

Chapter 23

10 Consequences Of Adolescent Sexuality

1. Pleases Satan.

Anything that does not please God pleases Satan. Because of a teen's increase of sexual desires and the desire to experiment sexually, Satan will use this area more than any other to make young people fall.

Remind teens that Satan twists God's purposes into his own. With Jesus the Devil used Scripture to tempt the Lord (Matthew 4:1-11). With our children he will use the Lord's design of human sexuality for evil intentions.

2. Loss Of Virginity.

Josh McDowell makes a great call to sexual purity by challenging teens through True Love Waits. He says, "What better gift to give your spouse on your wedding night than the knowledge that you saved yourself for him or her."

Explain to your teen that except in the case of rape, virginity is not lost, it is given away.

3. Doubt Of God's Forgiveness.

Teens say, "God can never forgive me. What I have done is too awful." They need reassurance that anyone who confesses their sin to God is forgiven (1 John 1:9).

If your teen has confessed to being immoral sexually, yet cannot feel the forgiveness of God then pray with him/her. Pray boldly and specifically for your child with whom the sexual act took place. After the prayer place your arms around him/her and give the assurance of your forgiveness and love.

4. Dealing With Guilt.

Hand in hand with the feeling of doubting God's forgiveness is the feeling of guilt. A teen can feel like he has blown it physically and spiritually for life. These feelings seep into every relational area and can affect grades, home, and friendships.

Call 1-800-458-2772 and get the pocket guide *When True Love Doesn't Wait*. This booklet will lead a teen step by step to spiritual healing after sexual sin.

5. Loss Of Self-Respect.

Ask your teen to tell you the most sexually active person at school and immediately a name will be given. Why? Because a consequence of loose morals is a loose reputation. And once a young person is known for that type of character he/she will live down to the perception.

Even after a sin, teens can regain reputation by allowing the Spirit to produce fruit through their lives (Galatians 5:22-23).

6. It Affects More Than Two People.

Parents, friends, the church and a host of others are hurt by promiscuity. A parent's ability is questioned. A church may become known as being soft on sexual sin. And all involved can be embarrassed by the shame that accompanies the stares and whispers of others.

Watch the movie *It's a Wonderful Life,* paying close attention to the scene where George learns what the world would be like if he never existed. After the movie talk about the way one life touches another.

7. Pregnancy.

Each year approximately one million teens become pregnant. From there they decide to terminate the pregnancy, give the child up for adoption, get married and have the child, or have the child and care for the baby with parental help.

Take your teen to an adoption agency for a discussion with a counselor. Getting to witness the possibilities that are present with pregnancy may help deter your teen's sexual activity.

8. Contracting A Sexually Transmitted Disease (STD).

A teen cannot have intercourse with a person without

the possibility of having contact with that person's previous sexual partners. It's daunting to think that a teen may not be having sex with one person, but technically with ten because of the diseases that could be received.

Surf the net, visit the library, or doctor and get information for your teen about STDs. Though the photos may be graphic, it's worth it if it will cause a young person to think before following the temptation.

9. A Haunting Past.

The memory of a first sexual relationship will never be forgotten among those who wear the name of Jesus. Even ten years after the act someone may step up and mention the escapade to a spouse or a child who thought their mate or parents were perfect.

Through some of your experiences, whether sexual or not, share with your teen the ways the past has followed you through life. Encourage them to live in a way that the past may follow with pride, not shame.

10. Puts Distance Between The Teen And God.

Although God doesn't turn away from us, a teen may feel like God doesn't want him/her around. Second, a teen may feel like there is no use to follow the Lord anymore since the sin has taken place.

Read Luke 15:11-32 together. Explain that God is like the father in the story who waited for his child; who hugged and kissed him when he finally returned home.

Dear Parents,

Having known Joe for some time, I could tell something was bothering him. He stayed after class Wednesday night and asked if we could talk. Although Joe was quite fond of the girl he had dated for several months, he knew what he had to do. He wasn't coming to me for advice. In fact, he had already made his decision and told his girlfriend. He broke up with her. He had to break up with her. Having pressured him for some time to engage in sex, Joe knew that was something he wasn't ready to do. He had made a decision to wait until marriage. I was not the first person to whom Joe had talked. He had first gone to his parents for counsel.

Kim was well into college. She had been dating a guy for several months, and had been faced with a similar decision. Each time she went out with her boyfriend, also a Christian, she was feeling pressured more and more to have sex. As we talked, she shared that if they continued to date, she was almost certain she would lose her virginity in the upcoming months. Because sexual purity was so important to her, she was not willing to put anyone, including her boyfriend, ahead of her convictions.

Things did not go so well for Carolyn. While in high school, her mom had made it clear her parental responsibilities ended when Carolyn graduated. In fact, when their relationship hit rough waters, Carolyn left home. Her downhill slide picked up speed when she moved into her boyfriend's home. Going through a list of boyfriends, she graduated from high school and strayed away from God. Carolyn has returned to a relationship with God after giving birth to a child outside of marriage. While she and the father soon married, that relationship has been rocky from the start.

Parents, God has given you a special gift. For eighteen years, you have the opportunity to help your children develop a foundation of morals and decision-making skills that can benefit them for an eternity. Your children will respect you for your honesty, teaching, and ability to listen. Keep those lines of communication open from an early age. When they face problems for which they have no answer, make sure your children feel comfortable talking to you. Bad decisions during their teen years can have devastating effects. Save them a lifetime of heartache by rejoicing with them in victory and walking beside them during times of crisis and decision. Pray for them. Pray with them. Point them to Jesus in all that you do.

> For His Glory,
> Johnny Hobbie
> Youth and Family Minister

Chapter 24

10 Tips For Maintaining A Great Mental Attitude

1. Stay Focused.

Whenever we begin a new project we tackle it with all our might but over time our enthusiasm can wane. The same is true in parenting. There will be times when you feel like the best parent on the planet, and then there will be times when you wonder if it's worth all the hassle.

Reach into your memory bank and recall a time when your family was doing great. What made that time so successful? Was it your attitude, patience, perseverance, or willingness to work at it? Whatever the keys may have been, reinstall them in your life.

2. Face Problems Head On.

When someone refuses to deal with a problem, we say they are burying their head in the sand. Some people feel that refusing to see a problem will make it go away. But ignoring a problem never solves it.

Deal with the challenge immediately. That doesn't give us permission to be impulsive; it does, however, prevent us from delaying and allowing a difficulty to grow.

3. Maintain a Moral Lifestyle.

We become like our focus. If we fill our minds with unwholesome images and sounds, our thinking patterns will reflect it, and it will show up in our attitude.

We invite immorality into our home through the Internet, television, music and reading material. In your home you may be able to set a specific standard that all will follow. If not, then install filtering software on your computer so certain sites cannot be visited. Program your television so certain shows cannot be watched.

4. Maintain a Close Relationship with God.

Think back over your life. Do you feel that your attitude was best when you were closest to God? Did you display greater kindness and patience? Our relationship with God directly influences how we treat others, especially our family.

Let your teen see and hear your relationship with the Lord. Let her hear you pray. Let him see you serve another. One of my fondest memories was the open Bible across the table from me at breakfast when I was a child. I knew what my mom had been doing before she woke me.

5. Remove Life's Negatives.

"Of optimist and pessimist the difference is quite droll, the optimist sees the donut while the pessimist sees the hole" - unknown.

If you are a person who tends to see a cloud on a sunny day, optimize your "see good ability." Begin with a thirty-minute period and make it a goal to see nothing but the good of life. Keep working at it until you see more positive than negative in your day.

6. Prioritize Family.

Our family often determines our attitude about our family. When your family knows that they are not most important after God in your life, their attitude toward you could be very poor. In turn, this will cause you to have a bad attitude toward them.

First, stop right now and ask God to give you the ability to show your family how special they are. Second, take out your day timer and schedule a special activity for them with no interruptions.

7. Surround Yourself With Positive People.

Enthusiasm is contagious so get around some positive people and allow them to rub off on you. Write down the names of two individuals to call today for a joy encounter.

Read anything by Zig Ziglar or Dale Carnegie. These two men have the ability to lead you step by step into a great attitude existence.

112

8. Set Goals.

Most people with nowhere to go usually end up there. When it comes to our teenagers we can't afford to hold a take it or leave it attitude. We need to have a specific target in mind while shaping their lives.

List three goals you have for your family or teenager. Write down the date for completion of the goal. Develop an action plan to make the goal a reality.

9. Walk by Faith.

There will always be times when we don't have the answers and don't know which direction to turn. Our faith in God should allow us to keep a positive attitude even in the middle of unsure circumstances.

Paul said in Philippians 4:11 that he learned to be content in all situations. He went on to say that it is by Christ's power that he was able to do all things. How has being a parent helped you to learn contentment? How has Christ been your strength in times of weakness?

10. Constantly ask "WWJD?"

What Would Jesus Do? Transferring the answer into a daily walk will alter your life and the lives of those around you.

Purchase the WWJD? bracelet if you have not already. Some saw this item as a passing fad, but the truth contained in that simple question can change your attitude any hour of the day.

Dear Parent,

The time it takes for your child to grow from infancy to adulthood will bring a great deal of happiness, pleasure and joy to you and your child. However, it also will present many difficult and trying situations, particularly as children reach their teen years. The goal of parents must be to handle these difficult situations in a way to avoid lasting harm, to either the parent or the child.

To us, it seems that accomplishing this goal lies primarily in establishing close relationships with your children and constantly striving to maintain open communications. Normally, a teenage child is fully capable of considering and understanding reasons for rules or directions given by a parent. It falls upon the parent to present reasonable explanations and to give sincere and honest consideration to any objection the child may raise. The Apostle Paul wrote, "Children obey your parents in the Lord---", but he also wrote, "Fathers provoke not your children to wrath". Remember, the parent is the adult in this relationship and must compensate for the immaturity of the child.

A parent is entitled to and should receive respect from a child. However, this respect must be earned. Your children must see in you the qualities you expect of them. If parents demonstrate a close relationship with God and a living faith, this will tend to instill the same qualities in their children. Review your life and try to live as God would have you live. Be kind, gentle, understanding and forgiving, and give your children the same degree of respect you demand of them.

Parenting is difficult. One must work hard to be successful at it. But in the final analysis it seems that a close relationship with God, and application of the principles He requires of us will bring success.

Sincerely,
Paul and Saundra Bozeman

Chapter 25

10 Tips Teens Said They Would Use As Parents

1. "Spend More Time With My Kids."
Forget the myth of quality verses quantity time. All children need attention and a lot of it.

"If I was a parent, I would set aside at least fifteen minutes three days a week to spend with my teen. I might find that I would enjoy it and would add more time later. Just fifteen minutes could change a relationship."

2. "Not Buy My Kids So Much Junk."
Many children in America get everything they ever want. There seem to be few limits to the amount of gadgets and gear that the average teenager is given.

"My parents seem to think that buying me things will get me off the hook from spending time with me or doing things that I want to do. I wish they knew how little those things mean to me. I want them, not things."

3. "Study The Bible With My Children."
Unfortunately, some parents feel that it is the church's job to teach their kids about the Bible and God. Yet, from early in Scripture the Lord gave this responsibility to parents (Deuteronomy 6:7-9).

"I don't know why most parents say studying the Bible is so important when they never study it with us. I am going to study with my teen."

4. "Not Allow Them To Watch Trash On Television."
Growing up I heard, "You are what you eat" a lot. It was a vain attempt by my mom to get me to eat healthy. Just as our physical health is determined by what goes into our bodies, our mental and emotion health is determined by what goes into our minds.

"I am not going to be afraid to tell my kids what they can and cannot watch on TV. There are some things I don't watch because of personal convictions, but my folk have no idea what I watch."

5. "Critique My Children's Music."

Like movies, music has ratings as well according to the level of explicitly. Create your own rating system for your household and listen to your teen's music before giving permission for him/her to listen.

A teen writes, "I know the difference between good music and bad music. I am not going to allow my children to listen to anything that will take them away from Jesus."

6. "Teach My Children About Finances."

Recently a lady in our congregation said she was bumped at a light by another car. Immediately a teenager jumped out and tried to get her not to call the police because of his poor driving record. He opened his wallet and offered two crisp one hundred dollar bills for the damages. The driver volunteered that his parents would provide more money if needed. What kind of lesson has that young person learned about finances?

"The reason that I don't know how to handle money now is because my parents never talked to me about money. I'll teach my kids to control their money, and not let it control them. I'm also going to teach them to give God the first and best."

7. "Help Them With Their Homework."

Help and *doing* are vastly different terms. Provide as much aid as needed for your child to find the solution on his or her own. Guard against impatience and the desire to do the work yourself so it will be perfect.

"My parents help me with my homework and it has helped our relationship as well. When they have the time to help with simple school work it makes me feel like they have the time for my real life problems as well."

8. "Show Real Spirituality."

As parents we can pray, read the Bible, and attend worship services, but to our teens that means little if prayer, devotional periods, and worship have little impact on the day to day.

"I want my children to be able to look at my life and know whether I am spiritual or not. I do not want to have to tell them. It's one of those things that is easy to say, but hard to live."

9. "Use Balanced Discipline."

What is balanced? What teens are asking for is consistent discipline. They expect fair discipline that is fair according to the offense.

"I want to be firm but loving. I want my children to know that I will not punish one way this time and another way the next."

10. "Love My Children."

Love, as Paul wrote in I Corinthians, is the most excellent way. It can cover a multitude of sins, mend the broken heart, and bring the sun out on a rainy day.

"I will love my kids with all my heart, soul and strength. No matter what kinds of problems they have I want them to know that I will always love them."

Dear Parents,

If I were a parent I would definitely use tough love. I would be strict, but not too strict. I guess I am saying that I would like to be balanced. I would trust my children and let them have a sense of independence and responsibility while they are growing up. I would try my best to build a good, solid foundation at my house. I pray that my children would know the Lord and I would take time to encourage them in everything they do. I would really spend quality time with my children trying to get to really know them as they get older. I would make them feel like they could come to me about anything and that I wouldn't judge them by their mistakes, but teach them how to learn from them. I would know their friends and make sure I know where they are and who they are with.

I learned all of the above from my two parents. They

have supported me in every way they could. They have shown love and appreciation for me ever since I can remember. I want to be the same way with my children.

Also, sometimes we get into a power struggles with you as parents. I apologize for all of us as teens, most of the time you are right and trying to do what is best for us and for that I thank you.

Loving Him,
Toni Fowler
High School Sophomore

Chapter 26

10 Verses Teens Should
Use To Decide On An Activity

Does the activity:

1. Follow The Example Of Jesus?

(I Peter 2:21) To this you were called, because Christ suffered for you, leaving you an example, which you should follow in his steps.

2. Keep You Away From Impure Thoughts And Deeds?

(Ephesians 5:3-7) But among you there must not be even a hint of sexual immorality, or of any kind of impurity, or of greed, because these are improper for God's holy people. 4Nor should there be obscenity, foolish talk or coarse joking, which are out of place, but rather thanksgiving. 5For of this you can be sure: No immoral, impure or greedy person—such a man is an idolater—has any inheritance in the kingdom of Christ and of God. 6Let no one deceive you with empty words, for because of such things God's wrath comes on those who are disobedient. 7Therefore do not be partners with them.

3. Maintain Your Innocence In An Evil World?

(Romans 16:19) Everyone has heard about your obedience, so I am full of joy over you; but I want you to be wise about what is good, and innocent about what is evil.

4. Always Imitate God?

(Ephesians 5:1-4) Be imitators of God, therefore, as dearly loved children 2and live a life of love, just as Christ loved us and gave himself up for us as a fragrant offering and sacrifice to God. 3But among you there must not be even a hint of sexual immorality, or of any kind of impurity, or of greed, because these are improper for God's holy people. 4Nor should there be obscenity, foolish talk or coarse joking, which are out of place, but rather thanksgiving.

5. Dwell On The "Whatevers?"

(Philippians 4:8) 8Finally, brothers, whatever is true, whatever is noble, whatever is right, whatever is pure, whatever is lovely, whatever is admirable—if anything is excellent or praiseworthy—think about such things.

6. Cause You To Think And Do Wrong Things?

(Matthew 5:27-30) "You have heard that it was said, 'Do not commit adultery.' 28But I tell you that anyone who looks at a woman lustfully has already committed adultery with her in his heart. 29If your right eye causes you to sin, gouge it out and throw it away. It is better for you to lose one part of your body than for your whole body to be thrown into hell. 30And if your right hand causes you to sin, cut it off and throw it away. It is better for you to lose one part of your body than for your whole body to go into hell."

7. Allow You To Hang On To What Is God's?

(I Thessalonians. 5:16-22) 16Be joyful always; 17pray continually; 18give thanks in all circumstances, for this is God's will for you in Christ Jesus. 19Do not put out the Spirit's fire; 20do not treat prophecies with contempt. 21Test everything. Hold on to the good. 22Avoid every kind of evil.

8. Set Your Mind On Things Above?

(Col. 3:1-6) 1Since, then, you have been raised with Christ, set your hearts on things above, where Christ is seated at the right hand of God. 2Set your minds on things above, not on earthly things. 3For you died, and your life is now hidden with Christ in God. 4When Christ, who is your life, appears, then you also will appear with him in glory. 5Put to death, therefore, whatever belongs to your earthly nature: sexual immorality, impurity, lust, evil desires and greed, which is idolatry. 6Because of these, the wrath of God is coming.

9. Encourage You To Pursue Righteousness?

(II Timothy 2:22) Flee the evil desires of youth, and pursue righteousness, faith, love and peace, along with those who call on the Lord out of a pure heart.

10. Urge You To Cling To What Is Good?

(Romans 12:9-16) [9]Love must be sincere. Hate what is evil; cling to what is good. [10]Be devoted to one another in brotherly love. Honor one another above yourselves. [11]Never be lacking in zeal, but keep your spiritual fervor, serving the Lord. [12]Be joyful in hope, patient in affliction, faithful in prayer. [13]Share with God's people who are in need. Practice hospitality. [14]Bless those who persecute you; bless and do not curse. [15]Rejoice with those who rejoice; mourn with those who mourn. [16]Live in harmony with one another. Do not be proud, but be willing to associate with people of low position. Do not be conceited.

Dear Parents,

Life is full of choices. Just this month I will make the choice of a lifetime. I am making the choice on who I will spend the rest of my life with. When I think about what advice to share on making choices I think there is one question that will make almost all choices in life clear. Will this decision glorify God? That is the ultimate choice. Throughout my life I have had many chances to glorify God in my choices, yet all too often I chose not to. Scripture tells us those who hunger and thirst for righteousness will be blessed. I praise God that His promises are always true. If we make the choice on a daily basis to honor God and put Him first, He will bless every choice we make. When we are in tune with God, the Holy Spirit moves within us to be our internal guide. In Ephesians 5, Paul challenges us to be imitators of Christ. He then says that to do that we must live as children of the light and find out what pleases God. I challenge all of you to make the choice to glorify God and find out what pleases HIM. In my marriage I will seek to know everything that will make my husband happy so that I can honor him. I challenge you to do the same in your relationship with God.

Pray,
Jessica Guy Coleman

Chapter 27

10 Tips I Want My Teens To Know Before They Leave Home

1. How To Have A Personal Relationship With God.

Relationships flourish when time and attention are coupled for the express purpose of drawing two people close. A relationship with God is developed the same way. Daily Bible study, quiet time, prayer and the like are all simple but productive ways to spend time with the Lord.

Mentioning the need is usually not enough for young people, so there are two substantial steps you can take to help ensure your child's personal relationship with God. First, model your relationship with the Lord. Make it visible and desirable. Second, provide resources such as a prayer journal, or an application Bible designed for your child's particular age group.

2. An Understanding Of God's Grace.

Adolescents need to know that grace is a free gift from God (some adults need to learn this as well). We do not earn it, or deserve it, but we receive it freely from God's hand. The death, burial, and resurrection of Jesus Christ presents the free gift to everyone who will believe on Him.

A trouble-free acronym to remember is G.R.A.C.E. = God's Riches At Christ's Expense. Have your child memorize that phrase along with Ephesians 2:8-10.

3. How To Truly Love Others.

Love is such a loose term in our society that we need to define it properly. I Corinthians 13 expresses the finest attributes of love such as keeping no records of wrongs, does not envy, hopes, endures, does not boast, etc. Did you notice? True love is not filled with the selfishness or dishonesty as pervades our culture.

Let's teach our children to love others in three ways. 1. Unconditionally. 2. Selflessly. 3. Without expecting anything

123

in return.

4. How To Unconditionally Love Us As Parents.

Is this possible? It is if we love our children unconditionally. Plus it does an injustice to young people when they are expected to adhere to a higher standard than we are willing to live by ourselves.

Explain that unconditional love means "I will love you no matter what. I may not like what you do or how you act, but I will love you regardless." That precise love is demonstrated to us in Romans 5:8, "while we were still sinners Christ died for us."

5. How To Use Their God-Given Gifts.

Take a few moments and write down the gifts you believe your child possesses. Ask yourself, "What have I done to help my teen develop these gifts? Have I become an encourager or a discourager?"

Once the gift or gifts of your child are determined provide opportunities for them to be used. For example: If your daughter loves to bake, set aside a Saturday morning and let her have the kitchen all to herself. Sure, it will become a disaster area, but the smile on her face will be worth all the flour on the floor.

6. Never Give Up.

Who hasn't felt like quitting? Not giving up is more about hanging on than about success or failure. You will hear something like this at times, "This college stuff is just not for me." Or they might say, "I hate this summer job, I'm ready to quit."

When the can't-go-on feeling overwhelms your child tell a personal story about a time in your life when you persevered and received a blessing. Talk about character development and how each struggle in life provides an inlet to future strength.

7. How To Cook A Meal From Start To Finish.

Teaching a young person how to cook may seem like an unnecessary task, but it will pay health dividends in the future. How bad can it get if they don't know how to cook? I had two college friends that ate cereal sandwiches at each meal. (Recipe: Two slices of bread and four tablespoons of your favorite cereal.)

Waiting until the final month your adolescent is home will supply few "culinary tools" so begin early. When you feel your child is ready, invite him or her into the kitchen to help with the meals. While you are at it, provide dishwashing training as well. Even if they don't thank you now, their future spouse will.

8. How To Handle Finances.

Before your teen leaves home teach them about three basic areas of finance.

The first part of their income goes to the Lord. You may decide on a tenth, which is ten percent, or an offering, which is anything above the tithe.

Budgeting and balancing. Check out Larry Burkett's site www.cfcministry.org for biblical financial principles.

Debt. Credit cards and other high interest borrowing can deplete financial reserves and make a person feel behind for years.

9. How To Wash Clothes And Clean House.

Dorm rooms all across America could be condemned if the health department was brave enough to enter. Instead of using chores around the house as solely responsibility tools, use them as well to teach the basics of household care. If children never clean house or do the laundry while at home, what is the chance of them doing it when they leave?

10. Home Will Always Be Here For You.

When a young person moves away from home for work or college it is critical for him or her to know that your door and telephone are always open and available. Although they want to make it on their own there will be times of disappointment and discouragement. Your open door policy will be a welcomed retreat for their tough times.

Dear Parents,

There are many things we would like for our child to know before she leaves home. Of course, the number one thing is for her to know Jesus Christ as her Lord and Savior. While I'm sure that the specifics of our individual lists may differ a bit in content and/or priority, I believe we share a common method for reaching these goals. Contrary to the world's expectations for teenagers, I believe we CAN teach our children what we want them to know. God says that with Him all things are possible, and that if we train a child in the way he should go, when he is old he will not depart from it. We intend to claim these promises! Far from parent experts we are! Whatever success we've had as parents, the glory belongs to the Lord. Three things have been the foundation of our parenting philosophy. Number one, always teach what we believe is within the will of God as expressed through His Word, the Bible. Second, have definite goals in mind with specific methods for reaching those goals. Write them down, talk about them together and with your child, do whatever it takes to have a vision for your children and keep it foremost in your minds and actions. The third is the most simple, but probably the most challenging. PRAY. I don't mean just "Bless my children, Amen." Really pray from the depths of your heart about anything, about everything. Be specific, be consistent, and be never ceasing. The question was once asked of us——"At what age do you think a parent should start praying with their child?" The answer is at the moment of conception. Raising Godly teens is challenging, and many would have us believe God would say "Anything you ask in my name will be done." We can raise Godly teens and guide them safely through those teenage years. With God ALL things are possible! We believe ALL includes a spirit filled Godly teen.

Loving Him,
Billy and Linda Segrest

Chapter 28

10 Tips For Developing Your Teen's Spirituality

1. Parents Must Have A Personal Relationship With God.

The way you as a parent model your relationship with the Almighty will enhance your child's relationship with Him. It is easy to talk about or tell your child about the importance of a relationship with God, but your example will always speak louder than any words you could choose.

In the past week what visual evidence has your adolescent witnessed of your relationship with God?

2. Assure Teens Of God's Unconditional Love.

John 3:16 says, "For God so loved the world that He gave His one and only Son, and whoever believes on Him will not perish but have eternal life." Whoever believes? Not whoever is perfect. Not whoever is good enough. Not whoever does enough stuff right. Whoever believes? That's as unconditional as it gets.

Set an appointment with your child to read Luke 15 out loud together. At the end of the chapter ask your child to list the ways God's unconditional love is expressed in each parable.

3. Surround Them With Positive Christian People.

If you want your son to be a good basketball player, you surround him with the best coach you can. If you want your daughter to be the best cheerleader, you surround her with great cheerleaders. The same principle applies to spirituality. If you want him and her to be spiritual, then you surround them with the strongest spiritual people. The decision to grow is still in the hands of the child, but the likelihood of following Christ is better in the right surroundings.

4. Talk With Them About Their Spiritual Lives.

This may be uncomfortable at first, but like anything else the more you do it the easier it becomes. Ask about their walk with God and about specific prayer requests. Allow spiritual discussion to become a normal, healthy communication process in your home. Soon you will find your adolescent sharing details and prayer requests without prodding.

5. Know What Is Being Taught In Your Teen's Bible Classes.

It is our responsibility as parents to spiritually nourish our children, but Bible classes can offer valuable support to our efforts. Why is it important that you know what is being taught? First, so you can apply the lessons they learn in the classroom at home. Second, you need to be sure that what your child learns coincides with your personal belief in God's word.

6. Discuss The Spiritual Experiences Of Others.

As you think back through the years there is probably a list of people who have made a great spiritual impact on your life for many reasons. Maybe it was a best friend's prayer life, or a co-worker's faith. Use real life spiritual examples from the lives of others to encourage spiritual growth in your child. There is no doubt that our children can learn a lot from New and Old Testament characters, but when they are able to place a face with the faith it can produce faster results.

7. Encourage Your Teen To Attend Christian Concerts.

What kid doesn't listen to music? It's a challenge to get their headphones off long enough to get the homework completed in many homes. Since young people will listen to music, let's encourage them to listen to positive music with God-filled lyrics. One of the best ways to introduce our children to Christian artists is by taking them to a live concert. It will allow them to see the performer first hand and connect with the individual or group.

8. Take Advantage Of Christian Camps And Retreats.

Christian camps and retreats provide a fantastic environment for young people to be around their Christian peers, and develop lifelong friends. Although some don't feel that camps and retreats provide real world experiences, these avenues do strengthen a young person's faith by allowing him to see the faith of their friends.

9. Teach And Model Forgiveness.

How good is your "done wrong" memory? Do your kids hear you repeat the same names and situations time and time again with bitterness? Or do they pick up on the way you forgive and forget?

10. Make Spiritual Development Fun.

When God doesn't seem fun, remember that He created an animal with a hump on its back, a squirrel that can float on the wind, a fish with no eyelids and you and me! So how can we move from religious rigor mortis to a celebration of Christ? By focusing on God's blessings and not on Satan's curses. As God's people we have to guard against coming across as if all evil is stacked on top of us. When we let the joy of the Lord shine through us our children will learn that life in Jesus is real LIFE.

Dear Parents,

When my two girls were young, Laurie and I read books and stories to them daily. We felt this accomplished at least two things. It helped them with their reading skills and they both now love to read. It also helped teach them about the Bible, since most of the stories we read to them were from the Bible. We reminded them that the people we were telling them about were real.

While we are still a work in progress as a family, we tried to start early to surround them with positive Christian people. Putting them in a Christian school was a very important move for us. More than that, we encourage them to develop friendships at school and church with other children we think are being reared with the same values. We make sure we know where they are, who they are with and if we don't feel good about them being around someone or going somewhere, we do not let them participate. We tell them why we will not let them do a particular thing or hang around a particular person. Sometimes Laurie and I seem to be the bad guys for our decisions, but that's not a reason to compromise.

One challenge for me specifically is that my girls aren't me "x" number of years ago. They are individuals, maturing at their own rate, and I can't really judge them by how mature I might have been at that stage in life. But, I do expect them to grow. I do expect them to develop a relationship with Jesus and to make more and more decisions that show they're growing in that direction. We try to help as we can, but many choices are left to them. We can, through current event type devotionals, and praying with and for them daily, help them to make better choices. Seeing growth is very encouraging.

Finally, it's not only important to help them develop a sense of "who they are" but more importantly a confidence in "whose they are". I feel their spiritual well being is my responsibility initially. Laurie and I have only one chance to raise our children, and we're trying to do so in a way that reflects our own recognition of the awesome responsibility that it is.

Sincerely,
Patrick & Laurie Gregory

Chapter 29

10 Tips To Help Your Teen Stay Committed

1. Give Them Responsibilities.

In other words the teen owns the task. When you give someone a responsibility it will be done better if you allow him or her to accept the role without standing over them. Assign the work and step back allowing the teen to complete it to the best of their ability.

2. Listen to Their Suggestions.

Believe it or not, there are times when a teen's suggestion is better than the parent's. That's not a knock on us; it's just that teens can come up with good ideas if given the opportunity. Listen to their advice and then give them the responsibility to carry it out. When they know that they are making a contribution they will feel better about the situation, whatever it may be.

3. Encourage Them to Use their Imaginations.

Winnie the Pooh is known for sitting upon a stump while thumping his head, "Think, think, think. Oh, brother." Parents often try to make their kids think in an analytical way (wired). Today's generation, however, thinks in nonlinear modes (unwired). By permitting them to think in the way their minds work they will stay more focused on their commitment and follow through with greater results.

4. Allow Them to Apply What They have been Taught.

Parents spend years preparing their teens to make the right decisions and take the right steps. But if they fail to provide applicational moments children may never learn the true lessons behind the teaching. If you are teaching your child about honesty test the lesson in real life. Present an opportunity for your child to deal honestly with you through an action. Afterwards review the importance of what has been learned.

5. Allow Missteps and Mistakes.

Young people will stick to their commitments when they know that failure does not hold punishments, but an occasion to reflect and become stronger. John Maxwell writes in "Failing Forward", "The difference between average people and achieving people is their perception and response to failure." Throughout history the most successful individuals have been those who failed initially only to reevaluate and renew their commitment.

6. Display Your Trust in Them.

Have you ever felt uncomfortable when someone looked over your shoulder as you worked? How did it make you feel? Like you couldn't do the job? Like they didn't trust you? Our children feel the same when we interrogate them about their trip to the mall or inspect their rooms with a white glove after they clean. Weigh the moment and choose carefully the time to interrogate and inspect. It may be the non-criticizing times that train our children the most.

7. Pick them Up When They Are Down.

Even if our teens have permission to fail they will inevitably feel defeated when their plans don't pan out. Not making the football team or not making as high on a test as desired can leave a young person in the valley. It is in those moments that their commitments can be exchanged for a quitter's attitude. In this crucial time use your words and actions to lift their spirits and give them another chance. Take the details of the situation and explain what good can come out of it.

8. Help Your Teen Set Goals.

Someone has observed, "A goal without a plan is nothing more than a wish." It is easy and more practical to remain committed to something that has a strategy associated with it.

9. Never Give Up On Them.

If our children refuse to keep some of their commitments, let it be their decision and not because we gave up on them. Painful words like, "I tried to tell you that you couldn't do it" sow discouragement in our kids' hearts. It also communicates that we never believed in them. They may try and try again only to end up on their backs, but when they look up it should be us that they see.

10. Be A Committed Role Model.

Do our plans and our actions match? Do we make verbal commitments but fail when it comes to their completion? Where will our children learn about staying committed? From us. When they see us keep our word even when we don't want to, it will convey what true commitment involves.

Dear Parents,

The task of keeping young people committed is an awesome task, one that cannot be done without the help of our Lord and Savior, Jesus Christ. Learning commitment begins at a very young age. As husband and wife, we lived commitment in front of our boys. First in our commitment to Christ. Daily devotions were an important part of our life from the time Joel and Phillip were old enough to begin looking at the pictures in a children's Bible Story Book. They were taught how Jesus will always be faithful to them and in turn, they must be faithful to Him.

In elementary school is where we reached a different level of teaching them to remain committed to the task. It was when the baseball teams were practicing on Sunday, or they needed to be at Bible Drill on the night of a baseball game. There were many times when, as husband and wife, we would like to have done something with friends or just by ourselves, but we were faithful to be at every athletic event or anything else in which they participated. All night Friday night we were in the gym watching basketball and all day Saturday in the gym watching wrestling. Those were wonderful days. They taught our boys commitment to family, commitment to a team, and a commitment to their goals, even when the going gets tough.

As parents we must teach our children that even in

the tough times we stay committed to the task that is before us, whether it be to a team, to friendships, to our family, or to Christ. Dear parents, love your children, not in word only, but in deed and time. The dividends are eternal. Our sons, due to the time invested on our behalf as parents, have learned to remain committed to the Task!

Reaching Out,
Donnie & Nonnie Owen

Chapter 30

10 Reasons Families Should Not Watch Trash On Television

1. Excess Violence Pollutes The Mind.

Over 22 studies show a link between TV violence and aggressiveness in children. According to psychologist Brian L. Wilcox, these studies show that television violence has the following effects:

Copycat violence: Some viewers directly imitate or reproduce aggressive behavior seen through the media.

Exaggerated fears: People who watch more TV are more fearful and paranoid of our world than those who do not.

Desensitization: Children who watch violent programming are less horrified by true crime.

2. Television Watching Cuts Down On Family Time.

According to "Money Matters" the average child watches 15,000 – 40,000 hours of TV by the time he is 17. He goes to school 11,000 hours and spends roughly 2,000 hours with his parents. Keep a family journal that keeps account of the amount of television watched compared to the amount of time spent one on one.

3. Creativity Is Suppressed.

Television allows our brains to shut down and receive information without weighing or considering it. Critical and rational thinking is not needed. Challenge your family to a three-day media fast. In place of watching television, use the time creatively for the good of the entire household. Write notes, plan a family outing together, or go out to eat as a family and get involved in...gasp...conversation.

4. Represses Physical And Mental Exercise.

I am sure that you have heard of the label couch potato." Have you looked at a potato lately? Three hours of television a day adds up to 21 hours a week. That's almost a full day of TV viewing. Begin by having your family slash their TV time in half and use the new time for exercise or mental activity such as reading.

5. Can Lead To Academic Problems.

As you can see from #2, the amount of time young people watch television is disproportionate to the rest of their activities. TV watching takes away from study time and is distracting during that time.

6. Causes Irrational Behavior.

According to a U.S. News and World Report and the U.C.L.A. Center for Communication Policy survey of 6,300 decision makers in the entertainment industry, more than half say violence in the media is a contributing factor to violence in America. Seventy-nine percent of the general public say entertainment media is a serious problem.

7. Misleading Influence Of Commercials.

What sells? Advertisers would tell you that sex does. What does this teach our children about sexual manipulation and selling themselves figuratively in order to get their way? For the next two weeks concentrate on commercials and the messages they send. Use your results to teach your children about the schemes used by the industry to shape their values and desires.

8. Influence Of Ungodly Role Models.

"Evil companions corrupt good morals," wrote Paul in 1 Corinthians. Who are our children's media companions? Listen to their language. Does it mimic a media model? Look at their clothing? Is it influenced by an individual with less than godly intentions?

9. Creates The Wrong View Of Sexuality.

A telephone survey released by the group "Children Now" reports that two-thirds of those polled say they were influenced sexually by television. Seventy-six percent said that TV too often depicts sex before marriage. Sixty-two percent said that sex on TV influences their peers to have sexual relations before marriage.

10. Arguing Over What To Watch.

A local survey of 100 teenagers revealed that the television shows to be watched is a continuing source of arguments in their households. As parents it is our responsibility to filter what comes into our homes and heads through media.

Dear Parents,

The media tells us that it is okay to be selfish, lie, cheat, steal and do whatever it takes to satisfy self. God tells us that anyone who wants to follow HIM must deny self and not lie, cheat or steal. So how do we do what God wants us to do in a society that is driven by the media? One of the things we have done is screen the types of media that comes into our home via television. Network sitcoms and movies are basically out. Shows with promiscuity, profanity and non-family themes are also out. Sometimes we goof and have to change the channel during a show; the remote definitely comes in handy! Screening TV shows has also led to some interesting discussions with our preteen because he wants to know why certain shows are unacceptable. Discussions have ranged from a Christian's perspective on attitudes to teen dating and peer pressure.

The second thing we have done is limit the amount of time the children watch TV during the week (the weekend generally is not a problem for us). This has been the real challenge for our family. My youngest child would watch TV all day long if allowed, so we battle sometimes about the time she has "actually watched" TV on any given day. The positive side of limiting TV time is we have more time for reading and cooking together, both of which she loves to do.

Besides monitoring the TV, we also keep a heads up on the music that our children listen to. Before they really developed an interest in music we had already begun choosing certain CDs and tapes (which happen to be of Christian artists) to bring home for "ourselves." The children thought it was pretty cool that we enjoyed listening to the latest groups. Now, it's a family thing to go to the music store and listen to CDs together.

By no means are we saying we have all the answers.

In fact, some days we are sure, we don't even know what the questions are. However, we do know that our children have been called to do great things; the only way they will be able to do those great things is to rise above what this world has to offer and trust in God. It is our job as their parents to prepare them for their calling.

Praise Him,
Jerome & Terry Dees

Chapter 31

10 Tips For Raising Mission-Minded Teens

1. Be A Mission-Minded Model.

Jesus said, "Come, follow me, and I will make you fishers of men" (Matthew 4:19). Verse twenty says they left their nets at once and followed Him. Jesus not only taught with His words, but His actions. Before He sent the apostles on a mission He took them on one. Starting with your next-door neighbor, SHOW your teen how to do mission work.

2. Make Missions A Family Plan.

More than anything this is a conscious commitment to missions. No one can do everything, but every one can do something. If mission activity is going to be a priority in your home each member must agree on it, and you must have an intentional plan or words will never become reality. The following tips will provide some suggestions for your planning.

3. Explain What It Means To Give Your Time.

Acts 20:25, "In everything I did, I showed you that by this kind of hard work we must help the weak, remembering the words of the Lord Jesus, 'It is more blessed to give than to receive.'" God has supplied us with rich abilities to be used (given) in bringing more people into His kingdom. Becoming a missionary does not mean a person has to give his life to a foreign country, but giving our time to our foreign culture.

4. Host Missionaries In Your Home.

How often does the church get fired up when the supported missionary comes to present his slideshow of the past year? Part of the problem is the average church member does not know the person or the people he works with. Inviting a missionary to your home will allow your family an inside look at the heart and the essence of a culture. You may be able to arrange some details that will make it possible to take a mission trip to the country he works with.

5. Go On A Family Mission Trip.

One way to do this is to use your vacation time and money and allow this to be the means of bringing your family closer together. If you are asking, "What's a vacation?" or "What's money?" you might want to tag-team with another family and help a church with vacation Bible school or inner city work.

6. Start A Missions Ministry In Your Church.

It may be that your congregation does not have a mission team or ministry. If you want your teen to be more mission minded encourage her to be part of organizing a team that will minister to others. She may want to begin by gathering others who are interested in missions to plan a project for your community. From there it may spread to the rest of the church.

7. Keep Ongoing Correspondence With Missionaries.

Write or email a mission's contact once or more per month. Make it a family affair by including each member in the writing and signing of the letter. Another option is to include personal contact with a member of the missionary's congregation. Perhaps a child or older adult could be useful in developing a deeper heart for God's kingdom.

8. Read, Watch, And Listen.

Stay current with the political and social details of the mission location. When you see a newspaper or magazine article relating to the area cut it out or copy it for the family. Focus tightly on any television reports dealing with the country of your missionary. Listen to the radio as you drive and if anything is mentioned regarding the area, mentally log the information and share it when you get home.

9. Give Money As A Family To A Chosen Mission Work.

When you ask your teen to sacrifice his money be sure to let him know that you are doing the same. In fact, pool your money and contribute it together. Some ways you can raise money for missionaries is through a family yard sale, car wash, or bake sale.

10. Do Mission Work In Your Neighborhood.

A Monday night community Bible study, or a Saturday afternoon cookout might be great starting places for a local ministry. What unique ways can you service your neighborhood? What would be simple and non-intimidating to get your family started?

Dear Parents,

Raising our children to be mission minded was not a goal from the very beginning. It is more the result of actions taken along the way. We have always been a family that participated in activities together. Whether it was school, church, or community, we have tried to include the children as much as possible. When the children were small, we took them with us on church wide campaigns. They thought the trips were as much fun as vacation. It was so good for them to be around other families who felt strongly about mission work. We focused on the fun of being with other Christians and the help we were giving to people who needed it.

Since the children have become teenagers, we have still taken an interest in the teen mission trips. We help the kids raise money for the trips and have volunteered to chaperone. We have seen what a life-changing impact mission work has had on them. Both children have been given the opportunity to be actively involved in the Inner City Ministry. Seeing children who have so little has been an invaluable experience.

Start early letting your child be involved. It is never too soon to let them feel a part of serving and teaching others. Talk about mission work with enthusiasm. Be involved yourself and show your child that it can be both fun and rewarding.

Serving Him,
Louis and Nita Hartzog

Chapter 32

10 Habits To Help Your
Teen with Stress

1. The Habit Of Proper Exercise.

Regular exercise is one of the best stress reducers, and most teens do not get enough of it. Sure, they have cheerleading and sports, but those are competitive processes that can add to the stress levels. How often do your kids exercise for health?

The medical community agrees that keeping fit not only reduces stress but also reduces the risks of heart attacks and aids in restful sleep. A basic program that anyone can start is walking for thirty minutes three times per week. Encourage your child to use this as prayer time or reflection time. As with any program, consult your personal physician before beginning.

2. The Habit Of Proper Eating Habits.

Does the balanced diet still exist? It does, but it requires more effort than the fast-food variety. Don't be concerned with a particular "diet." Just make sure the needed nutrients are available in your home. Fill the fridge with fruits instead of the cupboard with chips. Load the shelves with veggies instead of cakes and cookies.

Have your adolescents keep a one-week journal of *every* morsel that enters their mouths. Review the details and determine how you can make moderate adjustments. You don't have to cut out all the junk, but that may be the very source of their stress.

3. The Habit Of Proper Rest.

Most teens are like the Energizer Bunny, they keep going, and going, and going. The only problem is that the human body is not designed to do that. We must have our rest to function correctly and relate correctly. When is your teen the most cranky and least responsive? Most likely when the most tired.

On weeknights set a specific bedtime curfew. I know it sounds old fashioned, but it will help them function at school. On Fridays set a later sleep curfew with the stipulation that they get to sleep as late as they want on Saturday mornings.

4. The Habit Of Social Balance.

A teen's social schedule not only stresses them, it stresses parents. Pick up, drop off. Meet here, meet there. Check the watch...five minutes late...ten minutes late...half hour late...call the police station.

Friends, clubs, sports, etc., fill the calendar while challenging our available time. Create balance through healthy barriers by: blocking out time for family togetherness; limiting the involvement of your child to one or two specific activities instead of ten; or establishing a couple of nights of the week that cannot be interrupted regardless of the social event.

5. The Habit Of Time Management.

Stress comes when the day's events are a blur from beginning to end. Activities feel like they are back to back with no time to take a breath. If teens were to keep a simple organizer on them (even if its just a sheet of paper with the day's schedule) it would allow them to stay focused and more relaxed. They would see that nothing is scheduled between the end of school at 3:00 and play practice at 3:30. Just knowing that break exists can provide peace.

6. The Habit Of Self-Control.

Caffeine, alcohol, nicotine, even sugar can be addictive and create stress when a person does not get his "fix." All of those items can be detrimental, while alcohol and nicotine are two that we want our kids to completely avoid. The challenge is that most if not all of those substances make up the average teenager's life. They know the harmful effects, so it becomes more of a self-control issue than a knowledge issue.

7. The Habit Of A Positive Attitude.

"Rejoice always, I will say it again rejoice" (Philippians 4:4). Was Paul acting as the first motivational speaker? Not exactly. He wanted us to see that the Lord is the true source of blessing. People and politics raise stress levels and Paul wanted us to know that the joy found in God is greater than any negative found in the world.

Help your teen become more positive by becoming less badgering and more engaging. Sometimes our teen's bad attitudes come from our poor approach. When we confront a problem with the joy of the Lord (joy, not wrath) then the response may become more positive.

8. The Habit Of Honest Evaluation.

If your child is particularly stressed maybe it time to stop accepting his "I'll get over it" comment, and seek a medical evaluation. Of course, this is not the first step to take at the first indication of anxiety. Rather, it should be considered if an ongoing pattern develops.

Pride can get in our way when it comes to medical attention for emotional challenges. It is not a disgrace to go to the doctor for emotional problems any more than going to the doctor for a broken arm.

9. The Habit Of a Stress Test.

Here are some signs of stress that you can check from time to time.

Physical signs: unusual perspiration, abdominal cramps, recurring illnesses, involuntary muscle contractions, tension headaches, and stomach ulcers.

Emotional signs: panic, guilt fear, agitation, denial, depression, feeling overwhelmed, feeling out of control, worry, grief, inappropriate emotional response.

Thought patterns: paranoia, poor attention, poor judgment, nightmares, blaming others.

Behavior: difficulty sleeping, increased fatigue, withdrawal, alienated loved ones, uncontrolled anger and crying spells.

10. The Habit Of A Daily Time With God.

"Do not be anxious about anything, but in everything, by

prayer and petition, with thanksgiving, present your requests to God. And the peace of God, which transcends all understanding, will guard your hearts and minds in Christ Jesus" (Philippians 4:6,7). The passage clearly teaches, "Don't get stressed, pray!"

Dear Parents,

By the way of introduction, I just want to say, "Been there, done that." Sorry about using an old cliché but it fits so well. David and I raised our three birth children, 19 foster children of various ages, mostly teens, and all the assorted friends that visit and sleep over and went on vacation with us.

Teen stress rears its ugly head in many different ways. You may find your son or daughter generally more irritable and negative. They may complain about tightness in their muscles; they may have trouble falling asleep (trouble waking up is an "occupational hazard" of being a teen or it was in all three of mine); show an increase in nervous habits, such as biting nails, tapping fingertips, chewing lip, crying, etc.; or they may overeat or neglect regular mealtimes. This is just the tip of the iceberg!

Now that we have discussed some of the signs to look for, let us look at some of the solutions:

PRAY. Pray for the Lord to guide you and your teen in all decisions. Let them hear you pray. Let them see you read your Bible. I said bedtime prayers with all my children until they left home. Yes, at 18, one even reminded me when I went to bed before he did. I had to get up, go to his room and tuck him in. What a precious memory! Form habits early and nobody will be uncomfortable.

Try to stay on schedule. Go to bed at the same time every night and get up at the same time every morning. (Notice the bold "try".) Time management is a "biggie" no matter what age you are. Help your teen keep a list and prioritize events.

Keep a calendar in the kitchen with everyone's appointments on it so that no one schedules an appointment when you need to be at a band concert or whatever. Most teens want parents to be there-whatever the activity is. I thought that it didn't matter about some games until my oldest reminded me of every football game I missed. I repent.

Encourage everyone to eat a good breakfast and keep the right kinds of snacks on hand for nibbling. Snacks such as carrot sticks, fresh fruit, and even popcorn are great for a teen's appetite.

Talk. Decide which meals will be Family Nights and everybody must be present for dinner including parents. Some of our fondest memories are laughing and talking at meals. When relaxed, teens often let down their guard and talk more about themselves and their friends. I wish we had eaten together every night; we did from birth to age 12.

Each parent needs to spend time with each individual at least one time a week. One of my daughter's favorite memories is going to an oyster bar with her dad. It can be a walk, a trip to the mall, a bike ride, or shopping. Just be sure to spend as much time with them as possible.

Teens are sensitive about their appearance. Choose your battles carefully. Our oldest son had a "rat-tail." I hated it, but I told him, "It's your hair. Wear it however you please as long as it's clean." My youngest had long hair, same song, second verse. Add grunge clothes; clean but ratty.

"God accepts us where we are but loves us too much to leave us there." That is just the way parents feel about their teens. We accept our children; we love them, and desire the best for them. My advice is to love your mate. Let your teen see a "True Romance" going on at home. Many kids are stressed today because they think their parents are on the verge of divorce and they do not know who they will live with or where. Give your children the comfort of "Home, Sweet Home."

My husband, David says he got his best advice from James Dobson—"Just help them get through it; about age 20 they will grow out of it. Do not give up." Growing up is really tougher on them than it is on us. We have already experienced so much and know "This too shall pass." Be firm but flexible, be strong but gentle, and be godly but human. It is like the words of the song, "I see in you the glory

of the Lord and I love you with the love of the Lord." Keep
seeing the possibilities. Do not give up; they will grow up.
Maturation is a journey and a destination.

Simply put—the body needs food, rest, and exercise
to grow. The mind needs thought, meditation and dreams.
The spirit needs to love and be loved; for God is love. Our
social self needs friends. We need to help our teenagers
"increase in wisdom, stature, and in favor with God and
man" just as Jesus did in Luke 2:52. When spiritual,
physical, social, and emotional needs are met, there is little
stress.

May God bless you as you de-stress your own lives
and set a godly example for your teenager so he/she can de-
stress also!

In Him,
David and Martha Jackson

Chapter 33

10 Tips To Stay Close To God As Parents

1. Spend Quality Time With God.

Bible reading, prayer, and meditation are three ways to spend quality time with God. It has been said, "A chapter a day keeps Satan away." Constantly learning and appreciating the love that God has for His children will change your life. Talking to Him daily will deepen your relationship with Him. Meditating on the blessings God has supplied will fill your soul with richness.

2. Be A "Jesus Witness."

Do not be afraid to tell others what Jesus has done for you. If you have read, heard, or experienced the blessings of Christ, you can be a witness for Him. Let others know how much you depend on Him in time of need and how much you thank Him in time of blessing.

3. Be a Servant.

Luke 10:25-37 records the parable of the Good Samaritan. Here is a man who possessed a tender heart and was willing to lend a hand to someone he did not know. He put himself aside for the benefit of another. He shared his wealth and his compassion. He represents the total servanthood package.

In what way can you become like the Samaritan? Who have you seen others step over, while you need to bend over to help?

4. Attend And Participate In Worship.

Attendance and worship do not necessarily go together. Anyone can show up at the "appointed time," but that does not mean any worship is happening. John 4:24 says that God is seeking worshipers. So does He find us each day? Do our children witness our worship?

5. Teach A Bible Class.

You might be thinking, "Teaching is not my gift." Then maybe you do not need to lead the class, but assist the teacher. Either way you will be required to study and prepare. Often it's in our preparation to teach someone else that we learn the most. The process of reading and reflecting on a passage will allow it to become part of your makeup. And since God does not separate His character from His word it brings us closer to Him.

Teaching can be intimidating, so begin by talking with other teachers, taking a course, or taking notes on what great teachers do best as you watch them. On the other hand each person is able to teach about the thing he is most passionate about. Is your passion God's word? What is it that ignites your soul? That would be the best place to start your teaching ministry.

6. Give Sacrificially.

Sacrifice is a relative term, and not a term of percentage. If someone wanted to have a midnight meeting, I would have to sacrifice to get there. If someone else wanted to meet at 4:30 a.m., it might be their sacrifice, but not mine because I rise early.

Sacrifice means to give something up at a cost. When we give financially, what does it cost us? When we give time, what have we missed because of it? Giving sacrificially keeps us close to God because it makes us like Him. John 3:16 proves the point.

7. Give God Your Time.

Time is something we all have the same amount of, but how we handle it is another matter. Stay close to God by using your time for His glory (Colossians 3:17). Whether we are fishing, shopping, or serving let His light be seen through our lives.

Ken Gire, in his book *Between Heaven and Earth*, shares the prayer of a housewife who washed her dishes as if God would eat from them. She scrubbed her floors as if God would walk on them. Adopting this attitude will allow every moment to count for Him.

8. Entertain Guests In Your Home.

In an age of high-tech, high-touch is highly valued. Inviting someone to your home immediately communicates acceptance and welcome. Plus you get to know someone better in your home than on a church pew.

In-house hospitality reflects the spirit of the church in its infancy. In Acts 2:42-48 the believers spent a lot of time together praising God and meeting each other's needs. You can be the church by using your home as a place of encouragement and friendliness.

9. Invite Others To Worship.

Psalm 122:1 "I was glad when they said to me, let us go to the house of the Lord." A simple invitation to worship is a simple way to let others know that God is important to you and that you are glad to be with Him. Maybe the person will reject the invitation, or maybe she will receive an unexpected blessing from attending with you.

Make a "Most Wanted List" with the names of people you want to invite. Pray over them several times a day and wait for God to open the door.

10. Praise God 24/7.

If you really want to stay close to God then praise, honor, and obey Him 24 hours a day 7 days a week. Use every waking moment as an opportunity to worship. Use every sleeping moment to refresh your spirit for another day of praise.

Dear Parents,

What a crucial role parents play in the way a teen develops! Consider the testimony of three key witnesses. First, sociological research says so. According to the findings of the U.S. Department of Justice, Bureau of Justice Statistics, 70% of the juveniles in state reform institutions grew up in single or no parent situations. The U.S. Department of Health and Human Services, National Center of Heath Statistics concluded that when compared with children in intact, two-parent families, children from disrupted families are at much higher risk for physical or sexual abuse. Second, the children say so. In a survey of 4,000 rural Tennessee adolescents, Dr. Nick Stinnett of the University of Alabama asked for a list of the greatest needs of adolescents. The teen's top three responses were (1) strong family relationships, (2) being wanted, and (3) love.

Third, the Bible says so, "Children obey your parents in the Lord; for this is right. Honor your father and mother.... that it may be will with you and you may live long on the earth (Ephesians 6:1-3).

Yes, parents are the key players in the human development of their teens. Our teens are depending on us and we should accept that responsibility, even before we decide to start a family. When we stand before God, as parents, we should be able to tell Him that we did everything we could to develop our teens in a way that would serve, praise, and honor Him.

Serving Him,
Donnie & Sherrie Hilliard

Chapter 34

10 Virtues To Instill In Your Adolescent

1. Spirituality.

Spirituality may be defined as the state or quality of being neither physical nor material; Soul apart from matter; Unworldliness; Elevation of mind. Those terms are what separate a spiritual person from a religious person. The religious tend to feel complete by fulfilling a ritual, while spiritual people tend to focus on a relationship.

5Those who live according to the sinful nature have their minds set on what that nature desires; but those who live in accordance with the Spirit have their minds set on what the Spirit desires. 6The mind of sinful man is death, but the mind controlled by the Spirit is life and peace (Romans 8:5-6).

2. Responsibility.

Responsibility is more than handling a task, it means being held accountable to an obligation – no wonder teens don't like responsibility. Give your children a sheet of paper and ask them to list the ways they have shown responsibility. Second, ask for some ways that they would like you to hold them accountable for the duties you assign.

26For Macedonia and Achaia were pleased to make a contribution for the poor among the saints in Jerusalem. 27They were pleased to do it, and indeed they owe it to them. For if the Gentiles have shared in the Jews' spiritual blessings, they owe it to the Jews to share with them their material blessings.

3. Respect.

Like Rodney Dangerfield, parents get no respect. It holds the idea of showing honor and courtesy. "Yes, Ma'am" and "No, Sir" are terms of respect. Coinciding with the terms is a proper attitude. Sarcastic tones and rolling eyes don't match the right approach.

How do you teach respect? By keeping a high standard visible in the home. If our young people are not respectful of us, chances are good they will not respect other authority figures.

12Now we ask you, brothers, to respect those who work hard among you, who are over you in the Lord and who admonish you. 13Hold them in the highest regard in love because of their work. Live in peace with each other (1 Thessalonians 5:12-13).

4. Honesty.

Has your child ever lied to you? Ever cheated? Ever stolen anything? Ever denied any of the previous? It doesn't mean they're bad, or troubled, just allowing some of their sin nature to spill out. Like other spiritual pursuits, honesty must be instilled. That process begins with our parental example. Do we say we are not home when we get a phone call we don't want? Do we honor our promises?

8Finally, brothers, whatever is true, whatever is noble, whatever is right, whatever is pure, whatever is lovely, whatever is admirable—if anything is excellent or praiseworthy—think about such things. 9Whatever you have learned or received or heard from me, or seen in me—put it into practice. And the God of peace will be with you (Philippians 4:8-9).

5. Helpfulness.

Giving service or assistance to others is part of our responsibilities as God's children. Teens can do this by beginning with their talents. In what way does their natural makeup provide a way to serve? Pinpointing such will provide an automatic point to begin serving. The following passage provides the attitude we should possess when helping others.

2Carry each other's burdens, and in this way you will fulfill the law of Christ (Galatians 6:2).

6. Humility.

Humility is the state of being lowly in mind, unassuming, and meek. Of course, the opposite is arrogance and pride. Someone has defined arrogance as ego and ignorance combined. Humility, then, requires selfless knowledge applied for the benefit of all.

Christ humbled himself to the point of obedience unto death. To remain close with God our humility should be based in His sacrifice and lived through His strength.

3Do nothing out of selfish ambition or vain conceit, but in humility consider others better than yourselves. 4Each of you should look not only to your own interests, but also to the interests of others (Philippians 2:2-3).

7. Obedience.

This requires that we follow God's command regardless of the circumstances. Jesus did not want to die, but He was obedient. In Luke 2, Jesus' parents had a tough time locating Him (ever been there?). When they found Him, Jesus explained the situation and He went home to them and was *obedient.* As challenging as it may seem, teens are not given the option of obedience, it is mandatory.

20Children, obey your parents in everything, for this pleases the Lord (Colossians 3:20)

1Children, obey your parents in the Lord, for this is right. 2"Honor your father and mother"—which is the first commandment with a promise—3"that it may go well with you and that you may enjoy long life on the
earth" (Ephesians 6:1-3).

8. Self-control.

From what we eat, to what we wear, every decision calls for self-control. Because teens live in the moment and want immediate satisfaction this is major area of crisis for most families. They want the car keys now, the money now, the date now, the sex now, and the permission now. If self-control is not learned now many roadblocks lie in wait ahead. Discuss with your teen the vital areas of self-control, including sex.

3It is God's will that you should be sanctified: that you should avoid sexual immorality; 4that each of you should learn to control his own body in a way that is holy and honorable" (1 Thessalonians 4:3-4).

27No, I beat my body and make it my slave so that after I

have preached to others, I myself will not be disqualified for the prize (1 Corinthians 9:27).

9. Cooperation.

No one lives in a vacuum. It takes the ability to work and get along with other people to thrive in life. As you talk about cooperation with your children share examples of how you see them currently coopering with others. Have them share some ways that they have made a joint effort with someone that you may not know about.

⁹ Two are better than one, because they have a good return for their work: ¹⁰If one falls down, his friend can help him up. But pity the man who falls and has no one to help him up! (Ecclesiastes 4:9-10).

10. Patience.

Patient teens sounds like an oxymoron like jumbo shrimp. This virtue, however, will profit them throughout their lives. If they are not able to wait, or think before reacting, then friends and fortunes will be few. Spiritually as well, it is discouraging if a teen wants to be a spiritual giant without enduring the battles of life.

³Not only so, but we also rejoice in our sufferings, because we know that suffering produces perseverance; ⁴perseverance, character; and character, hope. ⁵And hope does not disappoint us, because God has poured out his love into our hearts by the Holy Spirit, whom he has given us (Romans 5:3-5).

Dear Parents,

"Responsibility" is a word that few people are willing to claim today. From our political leaders to the person who takes your order at Burger King, the name of the event of everyday living is to play the "Blame Game." How are we as parents to instill responsibility in our children when we live in such an irresponsible world? Now that is a question we wish we had all of the answers to. As parents of a 17-year old and a 19-year old, we often find ourselves struggling with that answer. So what are we trying to do in this area that seems to be working with our children?

First, we as parents have accepted the responsibility to raise our children. It seems like such an elementary response, but the fact is we regularly meet parents who have not accepted the responsibility of raising their own children. We often find parents who expect the baby sitter, the day care center, the church, the school, the government or their parents to raise their child for them. When their child does not conduct themselves in the way he or she should, they play the "Blame Game." It is our belief that you cannot teach a child responsibility unless you first are willing to accept the God- given responsibility of a parent to raise that child.

Second, with our willingness to accept responsibility, we then try to model a responsible life style in the presence of our children. Children learn responsibility by watching us handle the various responsibilities given to us.

Third, based on their level of maturity, we then try to delegate various areas of responsibility to them. We offer guidelines for the area of responsibility but we try to leave room for their own individuality. If they fail to handle an area of responsibility, we do not snatch the delegated area away from them but we try to work with them to help them overcome the struggle they are having. Failure to handle a responsibility is not a negative event if it can be used as an opportunity to train the child.

Fourth, as they mature and master an area of responsibility, we then try to delegate an even greater area of responsibility and help them work through it in the same fashion. The key to being successful at delegating is not to give them something that overwhelms them or is in an area that they are not capable of handling. Another helpful suggestion is to make sure that we are delegating to them and not dumping on them. We do not believe in delegating something that we have not been willing to do ourselves. To do otherwise is dumping and not delegating and no one enjoys being dumped on. You lead and train by being a good role model yourself. As with most things, being held accountable also helps insure success.

It is our prayer that God gives us wisdom in this process. As we accept the areas of responsibility He has given us, we pray that He will in turn give us the wisdom and strength to be able to raise children who are willing to accept and handle the responsibility given them.

Serving Him,
Ken and Jan Kilpatrick

Chapter 35

10 Questions To Ask About Social Events

1. Where Will The Activity Be?

The place of an event often reveals its nature. "John's parents are out of town and a crowd is getting together to watch a movie." That kind of statement should send off numerous alerts. Its not that you can't trust your child, but maybe you can't. Or maybe you can't trust John, especially if his parents are out of town.

2. Who Are The Chaperones And What Are Their Telephone Numbers?

No chaperones, no go. Does this sound too stringent? Maybe so, but wouldn't you rather err on the side of protection than permission?

The older a child gets the less he wants to be watched, and the more he tries to get away with. When you have the phone numbers of the chaperones, you can call at any time to check on your child. That knowledge alone will keep some teens on the straight and narrow. Who wants the embarrassment of their parents calling?

3. What Is The Transportation Plan?

This not only includes knowing who your teen is riding with, but if they are staying in the same place for the entire evening. A popular ploy by young people is to tell their parents where they will be for the first hour, then move to an unsupervised location for the rest of the night.

This allows him or her to share the first hour's details in the masked innocence of full disclosure. By having ALL the transportation plans, you can know where your child will be each moment. How will you know? By using #2 late in the event to make sure your teen is still present.

4. What Time Will You Get Home?

Curfew has never been popular with adolescents, but by asking what time they will get home they set their own curfew. Whatever time is set, stick to it and make it clear what the result will be if they ignore it.

Be awake when your kids get home. More than one teen has snuck into the house drunk while their parents dreamed the night away. Knowing that you will be waiting for their return will do a couple of things. First, it will help them guard their behavior when they know they will see you when they open the door. Second, they will know that you care enough to make sure they get home safe.

5. How Can I Reach You While You Are Gone?

This not only includes the chaperone's number, but the event's number as well. Or maybe your teen has a cell phone. Make sure it is on and charged before they leave so you can escape the excuses of "I didn't know it was off" and "The battery died."

6. Who Is Going to Be There That I Know?

Be prepared for the name of every kid that meets your approval. You can follow up with, "Is anyone going to be there that you know I wouldn't want you around?" This is a tougher question to run from since you have phone numbers and addresses of those in charge.

There may be some names you do not recognize so you may need their phone numbers as well so you can call their parents to see how they feel about the event. Will it embarrass your teen? You bet. Will it ease your peace of mind? Absolutely.

7. Do You Know What Will Happen If You Break The Rules?

After all of the above details have been set then establish the consequences of not following the plans. Laying out discipline ahead of time protects you and lets your children know that you are serious about the event. A lack of disciplinary measures does not prove to children that they are trusted, but that they can do what they want.

8. Will Anything Happen That You Will Be Ashamed Of Later?

This simple question will help your teens think through the activity before they go. It will also help them make a conscious decision to remain pure physically and emotionally before the event.

9. How Can You Use This Occasion To Let Your Light Shine?

Instead of making them concentrate on everything they are to avoid, get your teen thinking about what they are to pursue. Ask them to look for the one who is not fitting in and to befriend him or her. Suggest that they are to be vocal about their faith when not going along with the crowd.

10. How Did It Go?

After the activity ask how it went. Be prepared to celebrate if your teen is thrilled. Be prepared to shoulder a broken heart if something or someone at the event hurt him or her. This is not the time to lecture or scold, but a time to encourage or hold your child.

Dear Parents,

Knowing that good and caring people surround your children is a very big responsibility. Milton and I took this very seriously.

Even as early as elementary school knowing our children's friends was very important for us. Birthday parties and sleepovers were a dime a dozen. We always ask questions about these friends and knew who, what, when, and where.

Junior high school brought about new challenges. We tried to stay involved with their activities and again know their friends and parents. We really tried to focus on school activities because these usually were better chaperoned and had a more age appropriate time frame. Being involved as chaperones and planners gave us a better sense of what was going on in our teen's environment. Even if we were not attending the event we knew all about it.

We often talked about what kind of behavior was expected and what their rules were. They usually called when things ran later than expected and this was appreciated and expected. Things did not always work like they should, but we tried harder the next time. Prayers on their behalf went out daily for their safety and good judgment.

Our children are now grown. Our daughter (26) is about to be married and our son (23) and his wife are about to have their first child. They were and still are the center of our lives and God is the bond that holds us together.

Sincerely,
Milton and Carol Strickland

Chapter 36

10 Reasons For Family Forgiveness

1. Because Jesus Forgives.

Forgiving someone, especially a family member, who has wronged you, is a challenge. Our inward nature wants to exact revenge, or at the very least a little hurt.

As Jesus hung on the cross, He said, "Father, forgive them, for they do not know what they are doing" (Luke 23:34). He also said in Matthew 6:14-15, "For if you forgive men when they sin against you, your heavenly Father will also forgive you. But if you will not forgive men their sins, your Father will not forgive your sins." As difficult as it may be at times, it is critical to create a forgiving heart.

2. Forgiveness Is Commanded.

When it comes to forgiveness we really have no choice if we are going to do what God wants. Mark 11:25 commands, "When you stand praying, if you hold anything against anyone, forgive him, so that your Father in heaven may forgive you your sins."

3. Others Have Forgiven Us.

Can you recall when you wronged someone and received forgiveness? Do you remember the relief and compassion you felt? Recollect those same feelings when someone in the family needs grace.

Mathew 18:21-25 records Jesus' teaching about forgiving others. The man in the parable received great forgiveness, but offered none. Christ then warned His disciples about the consequences of an unforgiving spirit.

4. Forgiveness Helps Our Attitude.

Just like giving a gift at Christmas is a greater blessing than receiving one, so forgiveness blesses our souls when we extend it freely. When we are on a clean page with everyone in the household everything seems to go better.

'This is what you are to say to Joseph: I ask you to forgive your brothers the sins and the wrongs they committed in treating you so badly.' Now please forgive the sins of the servants of the God of your father." When their message came to him, Joseph wept (Genesis 50:17). His brothers' confession allowed Joseph to heal the fractured relationships.

5. Forgiveness Repairs Bitterness and Anger.

Peace and compassion flee the life of one who fails to forgive. Ephesians 4:31 tells us to "Get rid of all bitterness, rage, and anger..." That is impossible when resentment resides within you. The problem may not be what the other person has done; it may be the bitterness in your life. Remember; attack the problem, not the person.

6. Forgiveness Builds Family Trust.

As a kid, if I knew I would receive harsh punishment I always let my error be discovered. However, if I knew my mom would be forgiving I revealed my fault without being asked.
A loving attitude with forgiveness does not mean that the number of mistakes will decrease. It does mean that those mistakes will be handled with a spirit of honesty rather than a spirit of deception.

7. The Apostles Forgave.

The reason we have such a challenge forgiving is because we take things so personally. That type of attitude will always result in the bitterness and anger mentioned in #5. Let's take a lesson from the apostles. One example is in Philippians 1. Paul was in prison and some "believers" were making it even harder on him. Instead of becoming angry he praised God that the gospel was being spoken regardless of the motive.

8. Forgiveness Enhances Our Walk with God.

1 John 1:7, "But if we walk in the light as He is in the light, we have fellowship with one another, and the blood of Jesus, His Son, purifies us from all sin." Our purification is directly related to our ability to fellowship, and we do not

fellowship those we have not forgiven.

Is there anyone in your household you have not for-given? Is there anyone in your extended family? That is a significant question because our children hear the unforgiving comments we make about other family members.

9. Forgiveness Fulfills Love's Directive.

"Above all, love each other deeply, because love covers over a multitude of sins" (I Peter 4:8). Forgiveness is an extension of love. If we feel that we cannot forgive a person we trace those emotions back to a lack of love for them. We might say, "I don't hate them, I just don't like them." But the truth is we don't love them, and without love it will be impossible to cover up their sins against us.

10. Forgiveness is a Salvation Issue.

There are a lot of gray areas when it comes to obeying God; this is not one of them. As mentioned before, God says that He will not forgive us if we will not forgive others. Guess what the eternal result is for those who do not have God's forgiveness.

Dear Parents,

We have all heard it said that the greatest gift a father can give his children is to love their mother and that is true. I also believe that one of the greatest gifts parents can give their children is the example of forgiving. Forgiving ourselves and forgiving each other. Relationships often begin with three little words..."I love you". However, relationships and families are often sustained by the three little words..."I forgive you".

As the wife of a recovering addict, I have learned a lot about forgiveness. I have learned that it is sometimes very hard. Even though I felt that, as a Christian, forgiveness should have come easy for me, it did not. As a Christian, I felt as though I should have been able to quickly "forgive and forget". For me, however, forgiveness did not happen overnight. It has been a process that has taken a long time. I had always thought of myself as a forgiving person until I was faced with true forgiveness. To forgive Ed for his drug addiction meant forgiving him for many things. Ed's addiction devastated our family. We lost our home, cars, money, everything. Forgiving Ed for the material losses was the easy part. The wounds of his drug addiction ran much deeper.

Our children lost a lot and they too suffered. They were affected in many ways. Most of all, their dad, their hero, had failed them. I wanted so badly for our children to forgive their dad for all the bad things that had happened, that even when I knew in my heart that I had not truly forgiven, I acted as though I had. A friend of mine once told me to "fake it 'til you make it", so that is what I did. However, when you fake forgiveness, resentment only builds up inside and the healing never starts.

In the midst of all of our losses, hurt, heartache and despair, Ed and I began to turn to God. When we started bringing God into our situation, a metamorphosis took place. Our lives began to change. Oddly enough, the one who hurt me the most, Ed, began to teach me the most about forgiveness. I watched him lean on God daily for strength to get through his addiction. I saw him praying often for his own forgiveness. I saw a man truly repentant, being changed in a way that only God could change someone. Ed talked to me often about "staying in today", "living one day at a time", not "throwing good days after bad", and "letting go" of things I could not change. Ed had to forgive too. He had to forgive himself. Through his continued prayers and meditation, I watched Ed not only recover from his addiction, but I watched him grow in faith and gain an inner peace from his relationship with God. God has changed Ed in such a way that I went from not only forgiving him, but also striving to be like him.

For a long time I made the mistake of waiting for the hurt to go away first so that I could forgive. I have learned that forgiveness must come first before the hurt can begin to go away. It is the first step to mending hearts and healing relationships. Our family would not have survived without forgiveness. Our children have witnessed their dad forgive himself. They have witnessed their mother forgive their father. I also learned about forgiveness from my children. Their forgiveness of their dad seemed to come so natural and so easy. If they struggled with it, they never showed it and I never knew it.

It has been seven years now and the good days have far out weighed the bad days. Our children have seen us pull together and they have witnessed us rebuild our lives. I know that they realize we are where we are today because of God and because of forgiveness. All of our children are married now. No matter how old our kids get, there will be times when they will reflect back on our home and family. I believe that how we leaned on God during the hard times and trials have had a positive impact on our sons. In a very cherished Mother's Day card that I received from our youngest son this year, had handwritten in it simply, "Mom, thank you for forgiving". As I closed that card, I thanked God for another good day.

Forgiven,
Barbara Bice

Chapter 37

10 Great Family Activities

1. Family Night.

Set aside one night a week or month for a family night in
your home. Turn off the television and get out the board
games. There are so many games to choose from, but I'm
sure you can come up with one that everyone enjoys. You
might want to close out the evening with a family devotional, which may include a few minutes of prayer and sharing. Make it a fun night so your family will want to do it
again.

2. Hiking.

Millions of Americans are going to state parks and pri-
vately owned land to take in a day of hiking. Hiking is inex-
pensive (unless you buy a pair of three or four hundred dollar hiking shoes.) Hiking is also a great activity to keep you
in great physical shape. So get up, load up the family, and
enjoy the great outdoors. Occasionally stop along the trail
and thank God for the blessings of family and nature.

3. Camping.

Camping is one of the most popular family activities in
the U.S. Americans by the thousands are loading their
families up for a weekend of camping. Do a little research
to find a state park or inquire about private land in your
area. Camping is an activity which should cause cooperation among family members. The work should be divided
up so everyone can be involved. From putting up a tent,
gathering firewood, cooking, and cleaning up, it all has to be
done for the trip to be successful. The main thing each
family member needs to take is a great attitude. Make
camping fun so everyone will want to go again.

4. Get Involved In Your Teen's Sports Team.

I have known families who are really involved in their
teen's sports and follow them everywhere to watch them
participate. Always be an encourager to your teen no mat-

ter how well he or she does. Encourage them to do their best but don't pressure them until it is not fun. Thank God that your teen is healthy enough to be involved. Warning: Don't try to live your life through the life of your teen in sports.

5. Adopt A Classroom.

I am sure there are classrooms in your church that could use repair and painting. What better way to teach your teen to reach out and help than to actually get them busy doing something. We often sit back and see things that need to be done but very seldom do them. Teach your teen not to just be a "talker" but a "doer" as well. Find a room, set aside a Saturday or two, and get busy.

6. Visit a Hospital Or Nursing Home.

This activity seems so simple and yet it is one that we usually don't like to do. Some have said that going to a hospital or nursing home is just too depressing. How do you think the people feel that have to stay there for extended periods of time? Don't you think a short visit would lift their spirits? Push the point of putting ourselves aside and focusing on others to your teen.

7. Old Movie Night.

I realize that not much communication takes place during movies but there are several old classics that your teen may enjoy. How about "Ole Yeller" or "The Wizard of Oz"? These are classics which we all grew up with and may help in some way bridge the generation gap. Pop the corn and put in the flick and enjoy the night.

8. Family Skiing.

This could be expensive unless you live close to snow, but it could also be a trip that your family will not soon forget. Start praying weeks before you leave that everyone will have fun, be safe, and have a great attitude. Take plenty of pictures and you might consider making a scrapbook about the trip when you return.

9. Cookouts Or Picnics.

It would be great to choose one afternoon a month for your family to have a cookout or picnic. If it is possible to go somewhere away from your home it will be less distractions. Try to get away from television, telephone, and computers just for a couple of hours. Picnics are fun, so plan one and take off.

10. Weekend Trips.

Family vacations can be very frustrating if you are gone for a week or two. Nerves get on edges, teens want to get back to their friends, and dad may be thinking about things at his workplace. Make your trip a one or two night adventure if you are not used to going on trips together. Find a few places to go that everyone will enjoy such as the beach or the mountains. If possible, let everyone be in on the decision-making. Do not get frustrated if things do not go a hundred percent according to plan. Most families are not with each other for long periods of time so be very patient.

Dear Parents,

Just as you, we long to provide our children with perfect and happy lives. We want our children to have and enjoy all the good things that we enjoyed during our childhood, and we try endlessly to avoid the pitfalls and shortcomings that we feel we experienced.

We find ourselves consumed with providing our children with the "things" of life and live at a rapid pace filling their time with things such as a birthday parties, trips to the mall, church activities, late night cosmic bowling and the like. We feel immense pressure to be on constant guard for their protection, always anxious that our children develop self-confidence and the ability to be independent of peer pressure. It's no wonder that we feel overwhelmed and that our lives seem in constant chaos and turmoil. The larger the family, the more difficult we find juggling the demands for our time and our resources.

The irony of our struggle is that the harder we try, the faster our pace and the more difficult we find keeping it all together. We become frustrated that our families seem out of control and before we know it our children are nearly grown and we wonder from where their attitudes, their habits and their friends evolved.

In our family, we try to apply one of the basic management principles of simplicity. We've learned that one of the most valued gifts that we can give our children is simply our time. As Christians, we're called upon to be simple people by living a simple life in the fear and admonition of the Lord. For our family, this means that we should simply plan our time and our lives first around Christ and secondly around each other.

One way we spend time together is by worshiping together regularly and consistently. Attending worship together is our norm. Our children began attending worship services with us by their second week of life. Our children simply knew no different.

We get involved in our children's lives in areas such as sports and in their school activities. We constantly strive to encourage them and if they're involved, we make it our business to be in attendance. We are their greatest fans.

We travel together. Our children play school sports. Two play on traveling ball teams. We spend nearly a fourth of our weekends attending sporting events with them. We try to find time for other activities such as hunting, fishing, target shooting, playing cards, completing puzzles, or any activity that we can use to share time. Most importantly, we try to learn what's going on in their lives by listening and being very careful not to jump to conclusions or appear judgmental. We try to take advantage of every teachable moment.

It isn't easy! It takes time! Unfortunately, time is what most of us least have. Frankly, it requires a sacrifice. We sacrifice time at work and time doing things around our home. We sacrifice our hobbies and our interest for those of our children. I never read an obituary that said someone would be remembered because they keep a perfect yard or a spotless home. Rather, people are remembered for the time and sacrifice they give to their family and to others.

Raising children is not easy! Consider this point. If one grew up from the earliest age eating with chopsticks, would he or she consider using a fork normal? Early and consistent action on your part is the key. If your children grow up spending time with you, learning your nature and the applications, standards and experiences of life based upon the time they spend with you, how do you suppose that they will view the world? More importantly, how do you suppose that they will view Christ? All children learn from others. For us, the question was would they learn from us or would someone else's influence fill the void we left by not consistently spending time with our family? May God Bless you as you seek His will and blessings in raising your family.

Serving Him,
John & Ramona Lazenby

10 Verses For Parents
To Lean On

Proverbs 22:6
> Train a child in the way he should go, and when he is old he will not turn from it.

John 13:34-35
> A new commandment I give you; Love one another. As I have loved you, so you must love one another. All men will know that you are my disciples if you love one another.

I Peter 4:8
> Above all, love each other deeply, because love covers over a multitude of sins.

Ephesians 6:4
> Fathers, do not exasperate your children; instead, bring them up in the training and instruction of the Lord.

Colossians 3:21
> Fathers, do not embitter your children, or they will become discouraged.

Psalm 127:3-5
> Sons are a heritage from the Lord, children a reward from Him. Like arrows in the hands of a warrior are sons born in one's youth. Blessed is the man whose quiver is full of them. They will not be put to shame when they contend with their enemies in the gate.

Psalm 19:14
> May the words of my mouth and the meditation

of my heart be pleasing in your sight, O Lord,
my Rock and my Redeemer.

John 14:12-14
I tell you the truth; anyone who has faith in me
will do what I have been doing. He will do even
greater things than these, because I am going to
the Father. And I will do whatever you ask in
my name, so that the Son may bring glory to the
Father. You may ask me for anything in my
name, and I will do it.

Mathew 5:14-16
You are the light of the world. A city on a hill
cannot be hidden. Neither do people light a
lamp and put it under a bowl. Instead they put
it on its stand, and it gives light to everyone in
the house. In the same way, let your light shine
before men, that they may see your good deeds
and praise your Father in heaven.

Philippians 4:8-9
Finally, brothers, whatever is true, whatever is
noble, whatever is right, whatever is pure, whatever is lovely, whatever is admirable—if anything
is excellent or praiseworthy—think about such
things. Whatever you have learned or received
or heard from me, or seen in me—put it into
practice. And the God of peace will be with you.

Dear Parents,

As I look back on the past 13 years that I've been a
parent, I realize that the most important task I have is to
teach our children God's Word, and to show them that it is
relevant in their lives. In this world of darkness they need a
bright path to walk down, and it is our responsibility as
parents to lead them to it. Truly, His Word is a lamp unto

my feet and a light unto my path. Psalm 119:105.

Many times during the tough times, I have heard other parents say "Well, children don't come with an instruction book." As I've thought about that statement, I've been reminded of the times when my husband and I have given the children gifts. With all the enthusiasm and excitement they could muster, they would open the gifts and begin to play with them immediately. Soon they would realize that without instructions the toys did not work as they were supposed to. Frustrated and discouraged, they would bring their toys to their father so that he could read the instructions and make them work. Once the children were shown how the toys worked, they would go off happily and play until their hearts were content. Psalm 127:3 says that our "children are a gift from the Lord." I had to ask myself, would a wise, loving heavenly Father really give us a gift without an instruction book? Not a chance!!!!! He loves us too much! He wants more than anything to help us raise our children to walk in His ways and to dwell in safety. He has given us the BEST instruction book there is—HIS WORD! All we have to do is read it and apply it.

God has shown me through the years that He has a WORD for every situation we encounter. I recall one morning when our son did not want to get out of the bed. Still half asleep, he told me that God had told him that he could sleep a few more minutes. I laughed and told him that God never contradicts Himself and that in Proverbs 6:9 He had already said "How long will you lie there, O sluggard? When will you get up from your sleep?" Humorous as it was, it gave me another great opportunity to show him and his sister how relevant God's Word is to their everyday lives!!!

I encourage you as fellow parents to hide God's Word in the hearts of your children. "His Word will not return empty but will accomplish the purpose for which He sent it" (Isaiah 55:11). We can say many words many times to no avail but whenever we speak His words of wisdom we will not go wrong.

May God bless us all as we grow our children up for Him.

In Him,
Craig & Melinda Hopson

Chapter 39

10 Tips For Handling
A Family Crisis

1. Ask For Guidance.

Any crisis that you face whether family, job, or church related should begin with bold and sincere prayer. God has got to be involved when handling a major crisis. It is also good to ask others to pray for you, especially those who have had similar crisis in their own lives.

2. Face The Crisis Head On.

Meet the problem head on so you can put it behind you and move on in life. If you have a normal family you will be involved in several crises during the teen years. They may not all be serious problems but they do need to be dealt with.

Head on does not mean rash or rushed. When a crisis comes list your options and choose the one that will be the greatest benefit to your family. It may not be the most popular. It may not be the most severe. Make sure it is the best.

3. Attack The Problem And Not The Person.

How many times have you been involved in a crisis situation when the crisis is not even dealt with but the people involved are attacked from all sides? Usually when this happens the crisis is never solved and hard feelings exist and the crisis is often compounded. When dealing with a crisis, try as soon as possible to analyze the situation and think of ways to solve. Try to leave all personalities out unless they are the crisis.

4. Handle It Now, Don't Hesitate.

It has been said many times that if you put something off it only gets worse. That is especially true when dealing with a crisis in the family. Those involved have time to think of a way to justify their actions if a situation is put on hold for to long. Waiting too long can also communicate a lack of seriousness.

Most of the time it is better to put the crisis situation on the table with those involved present and get to the "meat of the matter" as soon as possible. A few hours may be needed to allow any tempers that are out of control to calm, or irrational behavior to be dealt with, but it does not require days.

5. Stay Calm And Use Patience.

Problems are usually handled quicker and without nearly as much frustration if you handle the crisis in a calm manner. A loss of temper only adds to the crisis. It is hard to keep your composure and use patience in the middle of a trying situation, but it really helps if you can. Pray daily for patience and for guidance in handling a family problem. There will probably be many as the years go by so begin now to prepare yourself in advance. Turn to God for peace and guidance.

6. Take It One Day At A Time.

It often adds to the problem if you spend a lot of time dealing with the past or trying to guess what is going to happen in the future. Deal with today's problems today and tomorrow's problems tomorrow. Handle them one day at a time, learn from what happened yesterday and then try to put yesterday behind you.

7. Remember, You Are Not Alone.

No matter what your crisis is there is someone who has had the same problem or one very similar. It may not be much consolation to know that someone else has had the same crisis as you but it is comforting to know that someone out there made it through it. Find those people and ask for guidance. Very few will refuse to help if they remember the feeling they endured during their time of storm. Don't be afraid to ask for help, it's out there.

8. Focus On The Positives.

Focusing on the positives that surround your family crisis will benefit the entire family. It will also let Satan know

180

that He cannot control your family. Learn from the mistakes made and vow to help others who face similar situations. Let your crisis be a positive learning experience no matter how painful it is. Being positive will help you to endure the pain and allow you to move on quicker.

9. Admit Your Mistakes.

It is not usually easy to admit your mistakes but if you do it will speed up the problem solving. It may be that you made a bad decision or said things that you should not have said in the "heat of battle." Whatever has been done or said in the wrong way should be dealt with and then move on. Just being able to say, "I'm sorry" goes a long way when you are dealing with a family crisis. Saying "I'm sorry" also teaches your teen that it is okay to be wrong as long as you stand up and admit when you have made a mistake.

10. When It's Over, Let It Go.

Now that you have handled the crisis and learned from it, put it behind you. If you hang onto the problem you are only going to be a miserable person. Why carry around a load when it's not necessary? Face it, solve it, and move on. Problems only last longer when you spend time dwelling on them after they have been handled. Why waste your time dealing with things you cannot change?

Dear Parents,

I grew up with the idea, if you did good all your life, always went to church, taught the Sunday School classes and were basically a good person, trials would never come your way. When a crisis came to our family I was not prepared. It brought me to my knees, but many lessons have been learned.

If you have never faced a crisis, get prepared. If you live long enough you will face trials in this life. It became very evident to me when trouble hit who was prepared, the one of us who had studied God's Word and prayed every day.

The foundation of God's Word holds the key to keeping your sanity. Prepare for a crisis while the waters of life are calm, so when the storms blow in, you will have a lifeboat to cling to. When you are in the midst of trials read the stories of Job, Joseph, and David. Read through the Psalms, you will be encouraged through these stories of those who have gone before us and the trials they went through. Pray even when you can't say anything but "Lord, help me!" God is listening.

Share with your friends your heartache. It may be hard at first, but realize that others will understand and may have gone through similar problems. These friends are the ones who will hold you up until you're strong again. There will always be those like Job's friends, who want to blame. Stay away from them. Instead surround yourself with encouragers, the friends who love you no matter what has happened in your life.

Go to church even when you can't do anything but cry. Back rows are for those of us who can't sing the songs without crying, for those who feel like God has hidden His face from us. Keep coming to worship, soon you will gain strength from those songs and from hearing the Word.

I remember someone telling me things could be worse, to be thankful. I didn't want to hear those words at that time, but I know now it was true. Take comfort that God will not give you more than you can handle. Look for the rainbows in life, the kindness of people, a smile, a hug, a card, or a prayer offered on your behalf. Look for those reminders that God has not forgotten you, He's right there beside you.

One of the verses that brings peace to my life is Isaiah 40:31, "Those who wait on the Lord, will gain new strength; They will mount up with wings like eagles, they will run and not get tired, they will walk and not become weary." Remember God's timing is always perfect.

God Is Love,
Johnny and Christy Johnson

Chapter 40

10 Relationships Parents Should Focus On

1. The Relationship With God.

The most important relationship that any parent can have is a great relationship with God. He is a parent just like we are in that He has love for His children. As parents we should constantly rely on Him for help as we parent our children. Many times we will be on our knees asking God to protect our children and show us the right things to say or do while parenting. Always rely on Him and give Him praise even when things do not go according to our plan but His. God gave His Son; could you give yours? How much time do you spend with Him in prayer and Bible study?

2. The Relationship With Your Spouse.

The relationship we have with our spouse is modeled for our teens. They notice how we handle things together, how friendly we are to each other at home, and how we treat each other in public. We also need to lean on each other as we parent our children. There will be times when we are not sure how to handle a situation, so we need each other to come up with a plan. Sit down with your spouse and make a list of ways that you can have a better relationship.

3. The Relationship With Your Children.

When we prioritize our relationships we, as Christians, know that God, spouse, and children are of most importance. We often have to work hard at having a great relationship with our teens. We spend time on our jobs, church activities, hobbies, etc., many times leaving our teens out of the mix. Again, with your spouse, sit down and make a list of five ways that you can have a better relationship with your children. You may think that a meal together one night a week is great, and it is. Write that down and come up with four more.

4. The Relationship With Your Church Family.

A church family is vitally important especially while raising your children. Most churches have a children's ministry, youth ministry, and a family ministry that works with parents in developing their parenting skills. Your church family is also important for support in times of need. There were times when our children were younger that it would have been very difficult to carry on without our church family. Make a list of the people in your church family who have meant a lot to you and write them a short thank you note.

5. The Relationship With Your In-Laws.

How sad it is that many families do not get along very well. Many times our children are caught in the middle of family squabbles and it is not very comfortable for them. I can't imagine a child being influenced by a parent not to have anything to do with another family member. Your teens will learn to get along with their in-laws by the way you get along with yours. Let your teens know how much you care about your in-laws, it will really help later.

6. The Relationship With Your Teen's School.

Having a good relationship with your teen's school can help in many ways. First, you will know what is going on and what your child is involved in. Second, if you are showing interest in the school the school will show interest in you. They won't hesitate to call if there is a problem or if they need your help. Third, it lets your teen know that you are interested in them. They may not like you being around school all the time but as the years go by they will learn to appreciate what you did, especially after they have children of their own. Make a list of ways that you can help the school, share it with your teens and the principal and get busy.

7. The Relationship With Your Neighbors.

Why is it so important to have a good relationship with your neighbors? You may need for them to watch your house while you are away or keep an eye on your teen for a day or so. Try to do all you can to help them when they need you. Your example teaches your teen how important good neighbors are. Why don't you make a batch of brownies and, as a family, take them to your neighbors?

8. The Relationship with Your Close Friends.

I personally do not see how people make it through life without close friends. Friendship is so important for many reasons. One reason is that very soon your teens will be leaving home to go to school, join the military, get a job, or get married. Another reason is that your teens need to learn how to relate to people outside your family. Teach the importance of friendship by modeling what a good friend should be like. If a friend needs your help do not hesitate to go and go cheerfully.

9. The Relationship with Your Teen's Friends' Parents.

This is another "biggie." Being friends with your teen's friends' parents is vitally important. You do not have to be best friends, but you need to be friendly enough to talk with each other about your children and what they are involved in. It will help in knowing how to get in touch with your teen and where he or she is. You will have a definite sense of security knowing the parents of your teen's friends, especially if they have the same parenting values as you.

10. The Relationship with Yourself.

How do you really feel about yourself? Your teens will be able to pick up on the fact that you have a high or low self-esteem. Their destiny in life will be somewhat determined by how you feel about yourself and how you face things. How you face your relationship with God or even how you face your parenting skills. Read your Bible daily. Also read motivational books by reputable authors who have a proven track record of helping others. Get plenty of exercise and eat right as often as possible. Study ways to make yourself better and get busy doing it.

Dear Parents,

Webster defines a relationship as a connection; kinship; friendship or a natural association. There are numerous relationships that we encounter throughout our lives beginning at birth. These all need nurturing whether they be between spouses, children, siblings, our church family our children's school, and most importantly our relationship with God. It is to a parent's delight when we see many of these relationships maturing within the lives of our children.

It was in the middle of the school year when my wife and I noticed the eating habits of our daughter had changed. She normally only had a small snack after school but suddenly began eating the equivalent of a meal upon returning home. We later discovered that she had been sharing her lunch money with someone less fortunate. How it warmed our hearts to know that the same young lady who at times could be defiant was growing up to be a loving and caring person. Our Creator made this a "We" world and meant for us to have relationships with those around us. My wife and I have tried to set that example by attending school activities, being active in our church and community, and building close relationships with those we call friends.

Jesus set that very example for us as He developed relationships with His disciples and those around Him. The Scriptures give us many examples of how we should interact with our spouse, our children, and our neighbors. The most important relationship is the one we establish with our Father in heaven. The relationship we build with Him is the premise from which we form all other relationships. If we, as parents, imitate Jesus in our lives, our children may also.

Our children at times are going to disappoint us; but just as you may think you are losing the battle, they pleasantly surprise you as if to say, "I've been watching".

Blessed,
Danny and Sandy Luster

Chapter 41

10 Tips For Recognizing Potentially Suicidal Teens

1. Previous Attempts.

When a teen develops a pattern of suicide attempts the following items in this category become even more significant and necessary to watch. Teens with a record of trying to take their lives lean toward repeating the attempt again and again. Although some feel that this is a cry for attention or love it cannot be ignored because an attempt may lead to success.

Tip: Seek professional assistance. Though that's common sense, it's possible for some parents to reject the idea because of pride or believing it's a phase of life.

2. Drugs And Alcohol Abuse.

Teens who show signs of depression in addition to links with drugs and alcohol consumption are at risks for suicide. Their feelings of inadequacy coupled with the availability of controlled substances present opportunity. They can consider pills or potions as a painless way to end their lives.

3. Rejection.

Adolescents who wrap their entire lives around certain events or people consider suicide when expectations and reality collide. They might feel rejected by a parent for never making the grade. They may feel discarded by a close friend. Perhaps they were told the starting position on the team was guaranteed and they didn't make third string.

4. Self-Destructive Behavior.

Reckless driving, advanced risk taking, and "cheating death" all are typical signs of those who are suicidal. They lack a respect for life, therefore they tempt death because they feel that either way they win.

5. Sudden Changes In Mood And Media Influences.

Suicidal urges often represent themselves in rapid mood swings, defensive behavior, and viewing and listening to media that glorifies death. After exhibiting this type of behavior, a teen may suddenly become at peace and act as if all negatives have been resolved. Sometimes the thought of the finality of suicide brings a peace and calm to the individual about to make an attempt.

6. Unexpected Crisis Or Trauma.

Surprise disruptions of life can trigger suicidal thoughts by rapidly placing a teen in unfamiliar emotional territory. The loss of a parent through death or divorce, moving to a new community and being rejected, the suicide of a close friend, and other distressing events frequently influence those who take their lives.

7. Communicating About Death.

When a teen writes poetry or songs, or talks about suicide or death in more than an inquisitive fashion, take this as a cry for help. Most individuals thinking about suicide use a variety of means to let you discover their plans without saying it directly.

8. Giving Away Possessions.

It's one thing to give away old clothes to a charity, it's another to give your best friend your favorite jewelry or other prized belongings. "I'm not going to need this anymore," has been heard by thousands of friends before a life was taken.

9. Withdrawal.

Suicidal teens often retreat from their friends, clubs, team, family, and the church. They shut themselves off from the world in order to convince themselves that they are not important to those around them. Their grades suffer, they shirk their responsibilities, and disregard their promises.

10. Guilt.

Guilt from sin, guilt from embarrassment, guilt from bringing shame on the family can induce suicide. Teens arrested for driving under the influence may take their life because they don't feel they could ever be forgiven, or because they feel they embarrassed their family. A person who is contemplating taking his or her own life may show one or more signs. However, Christine M. Sadowski, Ph.D., a child and family psychologist at Mayo Clinic, notes "...it's important to keep in mind that the warning signs are only guidelines." There is no one type of suicidal person. If you are concerned that someone is contemplating suicide — for whatever reason — arrange professional assistance for that person immediately. —Mayo Clinic Report

Dear Mom and Dad,

I'm sorry to be writing you this letter, but this is the only way. I'm tired of feeling like no one cares. I can't help that I'm different than what you think I should be. Dad, you never have time and Mom, you don't stop long enough to listen when I really need you to. So I have decided to relieve your problem. I'm sorry and I love you.

This note was written moments before a 14 year old took his father's 12 gauge shotgun, and ended his life in the woods directly behind his home. Sadly, the reality parents often come to know is too late. Children in today's society are troubled with pressures placed on them by peers and others that we as parents did not necessarily have to deal, nor are we able to fully understand.

Take time with your children, to understand to the best of your ability their needs and stand beside them, holding their hands when they face the peer pressures of today's society. Look for warning signs like depression, separation, or a general "I don't care" attitude. Never put off that "little talk" with your child until tomorrow, and above all else show you children you truly love and care about them and for them, just as God has shown His eternal love for His children.

Sincerely,
Michael Johnston
Undercover Narcotics Investigator

Chapter 42

10 Tips To Help Your Teen Through Your Divorce

1. Be Open And Honest.

Teens are perceptive; so do not try to hide things from them when it comes to family problems. Often parents will try to spare the feelings of their teens and this is a good intention but can be harmful in the long run. Most of the time it is better to be honest and say, "You need to know that we are having a few problems." Do not put the blame on anyone; just let them know that there are problems.

2. Assure Them It Is Not Their Fault.

Most teens will automatically assume that they are part of the blame so reassure them as much as possible that they are not. Being at fault is usually an initial feeling on the part of the teen and these feelings will often change over a period of time.

3. Never Put Your Teen In The Middle Of The Conflict.

Never try to make your teen choose sides during a divorce, or even after. Work hard to keep your comments about your ex to a minimum if you have to make comments at all. Teens need to be able to love both parents without added pressure. Also, never use your teen to relay messages to you ex. This has been proven to be one of the worst ways to put them in the middle of a bad situation.

4. Talk With Your Teen As Much As Possible.

Talking with your teen is vitally important while going through a divorce. They will need to have difficult questions answered and you will need to explain why things have worked out the way they have. This is your opportunity to be verbal with them.

5. Listen To Their Words And Feelings.

Teens have many questions and feelings concerning the divorce. There will be many assumptions made and questions asked. Most parents find it very difficult just to sit and listen while a teen vents but it is healthy and necessary to help with the healing process. Give them your total attention without interrupting with an answer to the problem.

6. Allow Them To Express Their Emotions.

Divorce is one of the most difficult situations that a teen will encounter. There will be times when they may cry themselves to sleep and wake up irritable the next morning. There may be times when their anger will surface and their actions are not acceptable. It is very difficult for a parent to know how far to go with letting them vent. However, there are things they can do such as cry or withdraw for short periods of time that are acceptable. Let them express their emotions but only to a certain point. That point would be that they will not be allowed to hurt themselves or anyone else

7. Assure Them Concerning Their Safety.

I have been involved in a lot of divorce cases when the teen would be worried about their safety. They worry about the dad coming and taking them away or a mom who has made threats of suicide or even burning their house down. Teens need to know that their safety is secure. If teens are not assured of personal safety it will probably affect their sleeping and eating habits, which will affect their school work and everyday life expectations.

8. Talk With Friends Who Are From A Divorced Home.

Parents and teens may gain a lot of insight from their friends who have gone through a divorce. There are people out there who are more than willing to help in a time of crisis so seek them out. It is very likely that most of us have friends, or friends of friends, who have gone through this tragic experience and do not want anyone to suffer the way they did.

9. Join A Support Group.

Support groups are one of the more popular and beneficial ways of seeking help for your needs. Most churches and community centers have some type of support group. A support group is simply a group of people who have the same needs as you. There are divorce recovery and teens of divorce support groups. Do not be afraid to give this avenue a try and know that you are not alone in your anxiety when meeting for the first time.

10. Get Out And Do For Others.

It has often been said that if you are out helping others that you will not have much time to deal with your own problems. There will come a time when you will have to face reality and realize that you are from a divorced home or that you are the one involved in the divorce. Whatever the case, helping others goes a long way in dealing with your problems.

Dear Parents,

We thank God for our children and that He has entrusted us to raise them together. We have three children that we are trying to do the best to raise in the evil world that we are living in. We have learned through the past 15 years of parenting that you can always learn something new from someone else that will help in parenting your children. As we continue to raise our children as Christians, we hope that what we have experienced as a blended family may in some way help you. Always remember to keep Christ centered in your life. Be aware of your actions, because children will do as you do and not necessarily what you tell them to do or not to do. Be as honest as possible; there were a lot of un-Christian things going on with the other family. Be honest enough to tell the truth even though it may hurt at first; we feel that honesty is the best. We tried to be as positive as we could about the other families, but can honestly say we did not always succeed at this because the other families were not Christians, their beliefs and morals were different from what we have instilled in our children, so this was hard for us. Also, always listen to and

193

for signs of trouble from the other family. We have always disciplined with firm tough love and we believe this is very important. We listen and love openly all the children the same. As you raise the first child things change because as parents you are living and learning. Be able to say I am sorry and that we too are learning about this parent/child thing. Always listen to what the children have to say-their thoughts and opinions are important. Never assume that everything is okay with your child. Always ask questions and be concerned, even if your child says you are being nosy. Be nosy and be involved! Always let your children know how much they are loved and needed. Don't just tell them, show them. Be a loving, kind, encouraging family! The most important thing that we can say as parents is to pray, pray, pray.

In Jesus,
John A. & Allyson A. Andrews.

Chapter 43

10 Difficulties Of Being
A Single Parent

1. Seeing Your Child Being Hurt.

One of the most difficult times for a parent is to see your child being hurt. We all know that along with divorce comes pain to the parents and the children. How do we combat that pain? We certainly need to bathe the situation in prayer as we ask for guidance from God. Talk with your teens and let them know that you understand that they are in pain and that you want to do whatever you can to help. Let them know that they can come to you to talk or that you will find someone for them to communicate with. Just let them know that you are there for them no matter what.

2. Loneliness.

If you choose to be alone that is one thing; but if you are abandoned, or divorced, that is another. Forced loneliness is something that no one desires. Along with loneliness comes a rash of peripheral problems. You may become angry, or even hostile because of loneliness. You also may face a sense of fear or anxiety. How do we handle these types of problems? It is not easy so you may have to force yourself into getting help. Set aside a time to go out and help someone else who is struggling with life's problems. You may try seeking out someone who is in a similar situation as yours just to give them a few words of encouragement. Fighting loneliness is not always easy but it can be done.

3. Not Enough Time.

It seems like that after a divorce you do not have enough time for yourself because you are always trying to help others, especially trying to meet the needs of your family. This is very unfortunate for anyone. One of the main things you need to learn is how to control your time instead of letting your time control you. It may be helpful to sit down and budget your time the same way you have to budget your money. Simply put your schedules on paper and try to make a few minutes of special time for yourself and your family.

4. Financial Problems.

Along with divorce usually comes financial stress. Oftentimes one or both parties will have to move down on the financial scale. What used to be a combined checking or saving account, if both spouses worked, now becomes one and this causes even more financial pressures. Just like managing your time it helps to write your bills down and begin a strict budget process until you see how things are going to work out. Probably in your church there will be a financial person who may be able to advise you.

5. Anger.

In most cases, when a divorce occurs tremendous anger takes place and this anger is usually directed toward your ex. This is common but should be avoided if at all possible. In many instances anger means that someone else is controlling your day and your attitude. You may want to seek guidance from a counselor or a support group if the problem of anger continues.

6. Accepting Your Ex's New Spouse.

After the divorce is final and time has passed one or both spouses may remarry. When this takes place it is often difficult for you to accept your ex's new spouse. When children are involved you may have to put forth extra effort to make things better. Do this for the sake of your children if for no other reason. How do you accomplish this? Of course, prayer is the main ingredient; you also might try planning your actions ahead of time. You take control of the situation and win over your emotions.

7. Leaving Your Child With Your Ex's Spouse.

This is very difficult to handle especially if you are the one who has been wronged. It is very important that you consider the feelings of the child and not necessarily your own, and that is tough. Many parents use their children to punish their ex-spouse and that is very dangerous.

8. Being Judged By Others.

I do not know how many times I have been told that a divorced person does not want to go to certain events because they feel like everyone is watching them or they feel like they are being judged. Even in Sunday school classes divorced persons may feel out of place because they do not have a mate with them. Many times they feel like people will think the divorce is their fault when it really wasn't. The reality of the situation is that you are divorced and that people will judge. Even though it is not right, it will happen. Try to go out with friends or invite people into your home for a night of fellowship. People who understand you and your situation.

9. There Is No One To Back Up Your Parenting Decisions.

It is always great to have someone to turn to and say, "What do you think about Johnny going to the mall Friday night with a group of guys from church?" But when you are alone you have to fight that battle by yourself and it is not fun. When you make a decision you have to deal with Johnny. Try to explain to your child the difficulty of making decisions alone. Will they understand? Probably not right away, but hopefully they will in the future.

10. Having To Make Everyday Decisions.

Do I pay this bill or that bill? Is it time to have the oil changed in my car or should I wait a week or so? What are we going to do about Christmas this year? Do we really need to go to Church today, I really do not get much out of it? These are just a few of the things that we have to face in our lives that are not related to parenting. Again, you may have to seek help from others until you get settled in to the decision-making mode. Being a parent is difficult, but being a single parent is even tougher. Always remember that you are in our prayers.

Dear Parents,

At nineteen I was pregnant with my first child after a teenage marriage. When we divorced seven years later I was pregnant with our second child. I raised my big girl and my baby boy without my second baby ever living with his father. I went on to get my college degree and became a teacher.

Then, hoping to have a two parent family unit for my children, I married again. This marriage had all the complications of stepfamilies and added many heartaches to both my children and myself.

A second divorce gave us another new beginning but a lonely one with too little time or money. My children had grown up moving many times with only me as their constant.

During these years, the sixties and seventies, the stigma of divorce was prevalent, especially in the church. However; due to my deep desire to raise my children as Christians, I disregarded criticism and accepted the fact that I had no support as a single parent from the church. My parents helped us, however, every step of the way.

I tell you this so you can see that I understand your struggles. I know your tears and tiredness. I know your nights--troubled and alone.

These comments are offered so that you can take hope. If you will seek God's face, He will work all things for good for you. It may not be on the schedule you desire, but He will prevail.

Today both my children are grown and have children of their own. I am so proud of them, not because they are beautiful or successful, but because they seek God and His will for their lives. If you saw them today, you wouldn't believe they grew up in a terrible turmoil. I remember—and I thank my God that we survived and pressed on the great Joy.

Stay Close,
Rebecca McCartha

Chapter 44

10 Difficulties Of Being A Teen In A Single Parent Family

1. Missing Your Other Parent.

Teens are often devastated by the fact that a parent is missing. A son could face the fact that his dad, who plays pitch or takes him hunting, will not be around as much as usual. A daughter could be devastated by the fact that her security is gone, whether it be Mom or Dad. This is usually a tough situation for a teen so allow them to see the missing parent as much as possible.

2. A Role Model Is Missing.

When a proper role model is missing out of a home a teen will suffer. Find someone in your church, community, or school who could provide this need. Do not be afraid to ask for help in this area, there are many who would be willing to help. There are those who came from divorced homes who know the pain and the needs of others.

3. Trying To Survive In Two Households.

In any divorce situation there is added pressure on the teen as well as the parents. Teens have to deal with surviving in two different households. They will live at one household and visit the other - probably on weekends. They may be expected to act one way at one household and act another way at the other. Try to make the living conditions as stable as possible at both households for the sake of the teen.

4. Dealing With Two Discipline Situations.

Another way that really hurts a teen is to be treated one way at Mom's and another way at Dad's. Again, for the sake of the teen communicate with your ex and try to have discipline problems handled in a very similar way. A teen will use you against each other if there is no consistency.

5. Dealing With A Limited Income.

When a divorce occurs it usually has financial repercussions. This financial problem will have a direct impact on your teen when they are used to living at one standard and have to adjust to another. It does not necessarily hurt them to make this adjustment; it is just different. Many teens need to live at a lower level just as a character builder.

6. Dealing With a Stepparent.

This is usually a very touchy situation. There are often times when teens will feel like they are letting a parent down if they treat a stepparent with a caring heart. Many times a teen will not want to be in the same room with a stepparent if it is going to make their natural mom or dad uncomfortable.

7. Not Enough Quality Time.

Let's look at a normal divorce situation. Dad leaves and Mom has to get a job or put in more hours at the job she now has. She has more housework to do, plus taking care of all the things that Dad usually did such as take care of the yard and the car. Naturally all of these extra details take away from family time. Make a conscious effort to build in as much time as you can for your teen.

8. Torn Between Two Homes.

How much consistency is required for a teen? I think that is a question for each individual to answer. There are teens who are not bothered by the "weekend shuffle" but there are those who are. The key word here is "torn." Make each home as identical as possible for the sake of the child. Making one home a favorite to the teen will only create more hurt.

9. Torn Between Parents.

The majority of teens love their parents very much whether they will admit it or not. They usually do not like to talk negatively about one parent to another in a divorced home. Special care must be taken not to use their broken spirits as a weapon against the other parent.

10. Uncomfortable Around Their Friends.

I don't know how many times I have had teens tell me how uncomfortable they feel when they are around their friends and they are telling stories about what their family did over the weekend or while they were on vacation. Unfortunately this is something they just have to learn to deal with. Is it painful? Yes. Is it their fault? No. Can they handle it? Yes, but they need to know that the parent understands their feelings of discomfort and is willing to alleviate them as much as possible.

Dear Parents,

It's those dreaded words that no child ever wants to hear. Some remember them vividly; others suppress the memory. "We're getting a divorce". Regardless if the parent ever says it to the child, at that moment a harsh reality begins to set in. Thoughts clutter the mind for weeks and months. But after asking the question "why" for so long, you eventually hit the "how." How will I cope with everyday life now that mom and dad are apart?

Hopefully you'll never have to say these words to your child. Statistics say many of you will, regardless of faith. I would like to encourage you with one simple but powerful word, "Love". Your child can get over a lot of things in life, even a divorce. But there is one thing he or she will never get over, and that is a lack of love from parents. Children of divorce may withdraw, go through rebellious stages, try to pit mom and dad against each other, or suppress their emotions, but all that can be overcome if you love them and love on them. I was fortunate enough to have that through my parents' divorce. Both of my parents would periodically wrap their arms around me to remind me they love me. Your child will relish in it, even if he or she doesn't show it. I've seen some parents try to cover up the hurt by placing material things in the child's life. Those things are all in vain though in the long run. What they will remember though is the time you hugged them tight and says, "No matter what we go through, I will always love you and this divorce will never change that." Please remember that, mom or dad.

Here is a final thought from scripture. In the midst of Joseph's family turmoil he tells his brothers what was meant for evil, "God has used for good" (Gen. 50). It took me a long time as a child of divorce to come face to face with this truth. Even when your child has been emotionally broken in the trauma of divorce, God can use it for good. It is unbelievable and unthinkable. But it happens. Finally in the rearview mirror of my life I can see how Satan tried to use it for evil. And many times it seemed as though he had won. But our God is bigger than that. Now I can see truths about marriage I might have never seen before. I refuse to enter into a commitment of marriage lightly or hastily. I know that a marriage takes constant attention and nurturing. I know I never want it to happen to one of my children. That's the good God wants to teach me. I honestly believe my generation has been so ravaged by the bad taste of divorce; we will rise up in protest with marriages that last and glorify God. May the Lord shower you with wisdom as you parent the next generation of God's kingdom.

God Bless,
Wes Gunn

Chapter 45

10 Tips To Help Tame Your Teen

1. Hug Them Daily.

I recently talked with a gentleman who was counseling a 17-year-old boy. The young man was in all kinds of trouble, none of which was of serious nature. In the counseling it was discovered that the teen had not been hugged since he was four years old. He had a handshake or two from his dad but that was it. After counseling with the father and him being enlightened to what the young man said he has since made amends with his son and things are much better. Hugging is not a cure-all but it is sure a great place to start.

2. Set And Negotiate Rules.

Whether you are struggling with your teen or not, rules need to be made and kept. It may be good to have rules written in a contract form for you and your teen to sign. It will also help to have in this contract what the punishment will be if the rules are broken. You can explain this by saying that a speed limit sign is put up for us to know how fast we can travel and if we break the law we will have to pay for doing so. Let your teen be in on the setting of the rules so there can be no misunderstandings.

3. Occasionally Do Things Your Teen Wants To Do.

This does not mean for you to spoil them. This simply means for you to do an activity that they are interested in. Skateboarding is not my greatest skill but I tried it one time because my son really enjoyed it. I can tell you that it bothered me at first for doing something that I didn't like, but when I saw our relationship grow because of it I was glad I did.

203

4. Listen To Their Music.

I cannot tell you what a struggle listening to my teen's music was for me. I really do not enjoy listening to something when I can't even understand the words and it sounds like a group of wild men beating on garbage can lids. Two things happened when I listened to his music. One, it let him know that I was willing to put my own feelings aside for the cause of strengthening our relationship.

Two, after I heard the lyrics to several of the songs I destroyed many of his CDs and refused to let him listen to that kind of music in our house. He eventually outgrew that music style and realized that we were not going to let him listen to anything that Satan was right in the middle of.

5. Never Reward Mediocre Behavior.

Reward when reward is due but do not reward for mediocre behavior. You may be thinking that this is a hard stand and maybe it is, but often teens can behave better than they do but will only behave at a mediocre level if they know they will be rewarded at that level.

6. Do Not Argue On Their Level.

It is never good to argue, but getting on the level of your teen is even worse. Usually when we get on their level the discussion goes from what you are talking about to who is in control of the discussion. In other words you leave the initial problem and more problems stem from it.

7. Praise When Praise Is Due.

This is different from reward when reward is due. When we speak of reward we usually think of some type of financial or a gift type reward. When we talk about praise we are talking about a verbal reward. It has been proven that encouragement usually reaps more positive behavior than does punishment. Try praising for the five good grades instead of cutting down for the one bad one.

8. Do Not Over Protect.

I read a note from a friend of mine which said, "If I had it to do over again I would let my child go outside with no shoes and shorts on a cold winter day instead of fighting with him all day about why he should not." Of course her point is to let them learn a few things on their own. Letting someone fail is often a better teaching tool than letting them succeed with the help of your input.

9. Model Unconditional Love.

No matter what the outcome of any situation is with your teen make him or her aware of your unconditional love. Are they going to make mistakes? Yes. Are we as parents going to make mistakes? We most definitely will. However, if we exhibit the same unconditional love for our teens as Jesus has for us, we will be in pretty good shape.

10. Call The Police If Necessary.

I do not know of any parent who wants to call the police to deal with their teen but it does happen. However, we should have the attitude and our teen should know that we have the attitude that we are going to do whatever we can to save their souls. If calling the police will keep them off drugs or out of any other type trouble, it will be worth it.

Dear Parents,

"No, that's not part of the deal," I told my 18 year old son on the telephone. My wife and I were going to be out of town for three days using a rental car and he had wanted to know if he could use our personal car to get around in while we were gone. Just three weeks prior we had gone through the agony of informing him that he was no longer permitted to live in our home. His reaction to that had been as expected; quick anger, cursing, a hasty bundling together of clothes and essentials, and slamming out the door with a rude gesture in our direction.

We would have been distressed even more than we were if this type of conduct was typical for him. It was not. Our son can be the most loving, funny; easy to be around person you would ever want to know. He likes lots of big hugs and kisses. He loves holding babies and playing with little children. He makes you laugh when talking with him. He is highly competitive at sports. And...he likes to have friends, lots of them, at any cost.

During the summer of his fourteenth birthday, his two closest friends moved away. This was devastating for someone like him, and was the start of the many troubles that would come. The "friends" he found to replace the close friends were smokers, drinkers, and drug users. It was not long before our son was involved in smoking tobacco, using marijuana, and other drug experimentation and usage. Our son began to change. Our inexperience had led us initially to believe that we were dealing with hormonal changes. However, over the course of time, we realized his behavior was not hormonal but could be correlated to what he was into at the time. Although our son thinks he acts the same way when he is not using drugs as when he is, we can tell an immediate and definite difference.

In four years time we went through an emotional roller coaster. There were calls in the middle of the night from the police. There was juvenile court. There were restitution payments, which we made sure our son paid. There were times when we thought he had turned his life around, only to discover that it was short-lived. His desire for the chance of having a close friend(s) usually would be the determining factor in whether to do right or wrong. Worst of all were the threats of suicide.

Finally, it was time for college. He would not be attending the college that we together had so diligently prayed and searched for. He would attend a college that we scrambled, at the last minute, to apply to. He had been recruited to play football by more than one college. We had turned down one offer to accept another. All of his expenses would be paid for. It was a wonderful opportunity for him in a Christian university that was ranked third academically in its region. His high school failed to get his transcripts in by the deadline. Another crisis had begun to play out. Although he is very intelligent and was initially getting all A's, he soon became a basket case emotionally after breaking up with his girlfriend and getting back into drugs. Soon he was skipping a lot of his classes. We heard more and more suicide talk. We had him come back home, thinking we could help him deal better with the issues if he were back with us.

After coming home he got a job in a restaurant. He was

always broke and complained he was not getting many tips. Although his attitude was terrible, he claimed he was drug free. He spent days at a time without coming home. He was belligerent any time we tried to find out what he was up to. We found out later, as we had presumed, that the cash tips were translated directly into smoke.

Finally, we had enough. He was going to be on his own. Initially we were going to let him use one of our cars to drive. Then we found out he was too young to get his own insurance and the car could not be put in his name. Since he had had numerous speeding tickets and three or four minor fender--benders, we were not willing to let him drive on our insurance any longer. We called him at work and told him we would be coming to get the car.

When he asked how he would get to work we responded that that was his problem. When we went to get the car there was a suicide note on the door. We were very afraid of what he might do to himself. On the other hand, we thought this suicide threat was possibly manipulation more than anything else. We have learned recently though, that suicide threats when made while a person is doing methamphetamines, are very real.

Eventually we were able to sit down with our son and come to terms with him. We told him that we were considering having him committed to a mental institution. The suicide note that he had written would have given us a way to get him committed against his will even though he is eighteen. We had already made the calls to find out what would be required to accomplish this, so he knew we were serious. He informed us that he had only written that suicide not because he was mad at us. Essentially we called his bluff, we think. We discussed other options also, but we finally settled on the following....

Once he can produce a clean drug test result, we will help his with transportation. It takes four to eight weeks for marijuana to disappear in the urine test and six months for other drugs to not show up in the hair sample test. We will also help him with college expenses when he goes back.

We have reserved the right to test him at any time. If he tests positive between now and college graduation, his car will be taken away permanently, and if he should continue to go to college, it will be at his own expense.

So far the plan seems to be working. Our son has finally taken up residence with two Christian singles that are a good influence on him. He is paying rent and he really does not have enough excess money to get into much trouble. Fortunately the Christian whose house he is sharing has laid the law down to him as well. Either he stays clean or he is out.

As parents, it was very hard to deny food and shelter to our own child. Even though we expelled him from home we still keep up with him the best we can. We take him out to dinner occasionally, separately and with the rest of the family. We continue to encourage him to go to church where he can associate with good people. He still wants us to do things with him for fun. He has mentioned that he wants us to go skydiving together. We would do anything for him that would really help him, even jumping out of a perfectly good airplane! We have also come to realize that sometimes the best thing to do for him is to do nothing. We simply pray.

Pray Daily,
Roger & Annette Wright

Chapter 46

10 Tips For Controlling
Your Anger

1. Do Not Hesitate To Get Help.

If you are out of control, get help immediately. In any situation anger will add to the problem therefore you are not dealing with the problem itself but with the problem anger causes. Although you may feel that you are not a violent person, unrestrained anger can lead to actions you may not expect and you will regret.

2. Admit That You Have An Anger Problem.

The number one way to overcome most problems is to admit that you have a problem. There is no way to overcome alcoholism without admitting that you have a problem with alcohol. Likewise an admission about problematic anger will lead you toward healing. Making excuses or rationalizing your anger will only steer you toward deeper and less restricted episodes.

3. Learn To Walk Away.

When you get in a situation that you know is going to cause you to lose your temper, just walk away, even if it is just for a few minutes. You are not dodging a problem by walking away; you are stopping another problem from happening. When you regain your composure you can go back and face the original problem.

4. Discover What Triggers Your Anger.

Another huge way to help solve the anger problem is to analyze yourself at the time you have an anger attack. What is really causing you to be angry? Are you angry with the kids for how they are acting or are you really angry at yourself for not handling things properly? When you dig down deep, you usually find something that you least expect to be causing your anger.

5. Take A Mental Walk.

Take a mental walk through your day and think about different situations. Try to figure out how you will react to something before it actually happens. In other words, how will you react if your daughter comes home and tells you she has been experimenting with alcohol? How would you react to your son who tells you that his girlfriend is pregnant? Learn to handle things before they happen. Do not spend a lot of time in a mentally negative world but do practice these suggestions.

6. Join A Support Group.

Support groups are a worthwhile avenue for anger management. A support group is a group of 8-12 people who have similar areas of concern. Anger management groups will get together usually one night a week just to encourage each other and share with each other. All of the members will have the same type problem. If your church does not offer this type of service contact the church in your city that is known for being the most socially active. If they do not offer the type of support you need they should have the resources to put you in touch with someone who does.

7. Talk One-on-One With A Friend.

Friendships are hard to beat, especially those who are willing to help you with a problem. Find a friend who will listen and give you constructive advice along with kind words and a shoulder to cry on.

8. Talk Directly To The Person You Are Angry With.

This could be dangerous, so be careful. You will probably want someone else to be present, not to back you up but to encourage you to remain calm. Do not approach someone if you know you cannot control your anger. If you have a serious problem with anger wait until you have gone through counseling or group therapy before you attempt to talk with the person you are angry with.

9. See A Therapist.

If you have a broken arm or toe you go to the doctor and he takes the necessary steps to heal you as quickly as possible. The same holds true with emotional problems such as excess anger. Go to a therapist and give him the opportunity to help you heal. Therapists are trained for these type problems, so do not hesitate. Also, do not be embarrassed because you need to seek professional help, just be willing to do whatever is necessary to restore your full emotional health.

10. Spend Time With God.

Praying or reading God's Word is not a last resort. Praying about your anger problem should be done at the beginning, in the middle, and at the end of your problem. Pray boldly and with faith that God will answer your prayers. Stay on your knees morning, noon, and night seeking wisdom from above.

Dear Parents,

As parents of two teenagers there have been many times when we've experienced much joy and happiness and there have been times when we've become angry with them because of their behavior. We've been very blessed to be part of a caring compassionate and God-loving congregation that has encouraged and prayed for us and with us along the way. We certainly don't have all the answers to handling anger but these have proven to be very effective and helpful when put into practice.

First and foremost pray, pray, pray, and pray some more. Staying in constant touch with God has really brought us through a lot of tough moments. Next, realize that if you get angry and if that anger is not handled in a proper manner, the situation only becomes worse. We've found that this will tend to make us all frustrated and everyone involved will either clam up or blow up. Thus causing the situation to either escalate or go unresolved and arise again at a later date and become even a larger issue than the original problem. It has really helped us to try to understand who or what the problem is that's making us angry. Sometimes we become angry over certain situations without having a clear understanding of what has actually taken place. Think about the effect that you are having on your-self and those around you when your anger is out of control. Try to speak in a calm voice, which is very difficult for us to do at this time but we are working hard on it.

We have tried something totally new to us when we become angry. There have been times when it really helped. Asking for outside help from another parent (tag teaming) often brings a completely new approach into the matter and sometimes the teen is a little more receptive dealing with a parent who is not upset with them. Find a friend that you trust and ask for their help, someday you will probably be able to repay the favor.

We have had to apologize to our teens on many occasions for mistakes we have made because of anger. Every time they have forgiven us and we are able to move on. Never be afraid to say, "I'm sorry" or "I'll try to do better next time." Remember, you are not only trying to set a good example for the present but you are trying to be the right kind of role model to make a difference in their future.

We really have a great relationship with our two teens. It was hard work for all of us but it was definitely worth the effort. Our prayers are with you, and remember you are not alone.

Serving Him,
Randy and Donna Stroup

10 Signs To Watch For To Know If Your Teen Is Becoming Involved With The Wrong Crowd

1. Disregards Family Rules.

Many teens, when becoming involved with the wrong crowd, will totally disregard family rules. If you tell them to be home at a certain time or be at a certain place, they may disregard your instructions. Often this disregard of rules is to show their friends that they are in control of their own lives and nobody tells them what to do.

2. Pulls Away From Normal Family Life.

It is not uncommon for a teen to pull away, to a certain degree, from their family. As teens they begin to go through a stage where they want to be independent and make their own decisions. During this stage they will pull away to keep from being told what to do or the family activities do not excite them anymore. This also happens when a teen becomes involved with the wrong crowd but to a greater degree. Take note of any drastic turns in attitude.

3. Begins To Lie A Lot.

Telling lies is a dead give away when your teen is hanging with the wrong group. They will lie about where they are going and whom they are going to be with. They will lie about having their homework done or even brushing their teeth. As small as that may seem it is a lie.

4. Clothes Style Could Change.

We all know that our peers and our environment influence our teens, as well as ourselves. We often change our dress style with the style that our society is now "in." The same holds true with our teens when they are involved with the wrong crowd. Most gang members are recognized by their clothes, whether it be ball caps, tennis shoes, or other forms of clothing. If you see your teen change styles do a little research to see what type of teen is wearing the type clothes your teen wants to wear. A change of clothes style does not always mean your teen is becoming involved with a gang or a bad crowd but it does need to be checked out.

5. Changes In Music Style.

Changing music styles is usually a dead giveaway. I have seen it happen time and time again. When a teen's music style changes it is often because of a change in friends. Many teens will change their style of music to be accepted by someone and not necessarily because they really care about the tunes. Listen to what your kids are listening to. If the music and lyrics are ungodly and unholy, ask about it, and why this style is so attractive to your child.

6. Becomes Very Defensive.

Teen's will defend their friends or become very defensive if you question their clothes or music style. It will seem like everything you bring up will cause a sense of defensiveness from your teen; they really think you are out to get them. Defensiveness is also a way for them to be in control of the situation.

7. Will Not Give You A Straight Answer.

As a parent the main way to find out how your teen is doing or what's going on in his life is to ask questions. Getting straight answers out of teens is really hard, especially if they are trying to hide bad relationships. More than just lying, they become evasive. They disappear without saying they are going out. They hang up the phone suddenly when you enter the room.

8. Their Friends Will Not Hang Around Your House.

The last thing a teen wants to do is introduce you to their friends especially if their friends, are a bad influence on them. One on one, your teen may feel like he or she can control the situation, but with their friends around they know they can't control everything said and done.

9. They Pull Away From Church.

When a teen becomes involved with the wrong crowd he/she usually pulls away from the things that are most important. They begin to make excuses about why they do not want to go to church anymore. They say things like, "Those people are a bunch of geeks or I just don't fit in there anymore." All of a sudden the Bible classes and worship service becomes very boring to them and the church ceases to meet their needs.

10. They Disregard Authority.

Most teens will disregard all authority when their lifestyle changes. They do not want to listen to their parents or teachers at school. They do not want to listen to what is said at church or by those in authority. At certain points they even begin to disregard the laws, not only of God but also of the land.

Dear Parents,

As parents of a teenager we have been through many, many trying times. We know what it is to wonder if you are making the right decisions for your teen. As long as you have your teen's best interest at heart, their safety and their soul, you are at least trying to make the right decisions.

There are many changes that we noticed around the same time that our teen started to become involved with the wrong crowd. Her grades began to decline and her behavior started to worsen. She was, for the most part, very hard to communicate with. At one time she was very interested in sports and other school activities but that interest began to decline. She began to disrespect us as parents and seemed to fight authority in other places as well. She did not want to follow any rules at home or school. What was once a very pleasant child had turned into a teen that was very hard to deal with.

Where are we now? We never stopped trying. We never stopped searching for ways to get our daughter back on track. I am happy to report to you that she is now doing much better. She is really involved in church activities and our problems at home are minimal. We have made a commitment to stay on top of all situations, to communicate as a family, and to stay involved with our church family, which has been there to support us all the way.

Thanks,
Rocco and Betty Arnold

Chapter 48

10 Tips To Teach Your Teen Responsibility

1. Model Responsibility.

If our teens do not see us as responsible adults they will not think we are serious when we try to get them to be responsible. Sit down and talk with them about the responsibilities of being a parent. Tell them what you are trying to accomplish. Share with them the pressures of being a parent. Also, share with them the responsibilities of being a teen in today's society. Let them see you doing responsible things in the home, church and work place.

2. Begin As Young As Possible.

As soon as they are able to comprehend start teaching them the concept of responsibility. They need to know that they have to pick up their toys or they will not be able to play with them tomorrow. Even at a young age do not give them everything they want. Make them do some kind of chores to get the "extras" such as a toy when it's not their birthday or Christmas. A little work never hurt anyone, not even a child.

3. Allow Failures.

It is okay to fail as long as they are trying. Thomas Edison failed over and over again before he invented lights. It took doctors years to come up with cures for different illnesses, but they stayed with it and were very successful. The apostles failed many times while learning from Jesus. The apostle Peter failed right at the end of the life of Christ, but he persevered and continued on. We have all made many mistakes in trying to raise our children. We probably learned more from our failures than from our accomplishments.

4. Encourage Decision Making.

Allow your teens and preteens to make as many decisions as possible. Let them tell you why they want to do something before you tell them "no." They probably will still want to do what they had planned, but they also learned a lesson, which will be applied later on in life. They will not always make the right decision, but at least give them a shot.

5. Begin By Doing Chores With Them.

You will have to show them how to mow the lawn the first time or fold a load of clothes. The best way to teach them is by doing the chores with them. Teach them how to work. Show them how and why you do the hard chores first instead of last. Teach the importance of doing things right the first time instead of having to spend more time doing them over again. However, they may have to learn the hard way, do it over.

6. Create Opportunities To Show Responsibility.

Create ways for your teen to show that he or she is responsible. You might try telling one time that they have to be home by eleven. Do not threaten or let them know what the consequences will be for coming in past curfew if you have already told them. Let them go and show their responsibility by being home on time. Tell them they have to make their beds everyday and take out the garbage when they see the container is full. Don't keep reminding them just let them do it.

7. Set Time Limits On Tasks

"You have thirty minutes to get your room clean." "You have to be through mowing the lawn before you can go with your friends." "Get done with your homework before you watch television." "It's nine o'clock and I want you to have this list of chores done by noon." These are just a few examples of setting time limits.

8. Do Not Accept Average.

Our teens will be below average or average if we allow them to be below average or average. There may be times when a teen makes below average grades, but he or she does not have to be below average in effort. If you have a strong work ethic you will never have to worry about getting a job. It may not be the job you want but it will be a job. Never accept average effort.

9. Teach Them That Their Decisions Affect Others.

Teens begin to mature in the area of responsibility when they finally realize that their decisions affect others. If they decide to drink they could take the life of an innocent person if they get behind the wheel of an automobile. If they decide to get on drugs and become an addict they may not be able to hold down a job so they get on food stamps or the government will have to provide treatment for them at the taxpayers' expense. Yes, most decisions affect more than just themselves.

10. Praise Accomplishments.

I have always been told that the power of praise is the greatest power that we can use while raising our teens. Compliment them on a job well done. Write them a note telling them what a great job they did accomplishing a certain task. Being positive gets a lot more accomplished than being negative with most teens. Unfortunately many times we look at the one thing they did wrong instead of the ten things they did right. Pat them on the back, hug their neck, let them know that you are proud of them.

Dear Parents,

As you read this, your children may be approaching the age of leaving home to attend college, get married or begin a new job. On the other hand, they may still be quite young as is evidenced by rooms cluttered with toys, noise levels rivaling that of a freight train, or sky-high orthodontist bills. In your mind, you may wonder if you will ever live to see them grown and able to function independently of your time, security, and the contents of your wallet.

Before you can imagine (and you know this if your children are grown), the rooms will remain devoid of the clutter of toys, walls will echo with silence, and the money you spent on straightening teeth will now be used for college educations and weddings. We have witnessed these transitions with our own five children and have struggled to cope with our nest becoming much too empty in the latter years.

One thing that has eased our letting go is watching our children assume responsibility for themselves as young adults and then as parents in their own homes. We have watched how they have handled their successes and their failures thus far. Observing them working through the good, as well as the bad times and coming out stronger adults because of these life experiences, has given us a sense of peace and has made the letting go process much easier.

We cannot dispense a magical formula for teaching children how to assume responsibility. We are keenly aware that each child is unique in personality and temperament. At the same time, we feel strongly that there have been definite principles and factors, which played a large part in preparing the children to become responsible adults.

At an early age, we gave the children age-appropriate tasks around the house. The children had to make their beds and pick up their toys. As they grew, they had the jobs of dusting, vacuuming, cutting grass, etc. The girls all learned to put a balanced meal on the table and all the children learned to do the laundry in preparation for their going off to college.

With a large family, they learned to take turns and wait for new shoes, much-wanted toys, or the latest fashion fads. When they became old enough to drive, they acquired jobs to help pay for their cars, gasoline and car insurance. All five have obtained college degrees, or are enrolled in college, and likewise, they have paid for much of their education themselves. By helping financially with their expenses as they grew, they became more responsible for themselves as well as their actions. Through hard work and perseverance, they were made aware that with freedoms and opportunities also came responsibilities.

We also tried to model being responsible adults ourselves. We inherently believed that unless we set the example, we could not expect our children to become that which we were not. The children observed as we both worked hard whether as professionals or as parents. They did not see us give up or succumb to the feeling of being victimized as we suffered two failed businesses during a recession as well as the loss of our four parents all in the same time period.

Becoming responsible adults will not free children of the ups and downs of life, but it will equip them with the inner strength and coping skill with which to handle these difficult periods. We hope our own children have observed that God has always been an ever-abiding constant in our life when all else was unstable. We hope they have seen Him walking hand in hand with us in the valleys, yet meeting us on the mountaintops of life as well.

King Solomon tells us in Proverbs 10:4, "Lazy hands make a man poor, but diligent hands bring wealth (NIV)." Our family may never be wealthy from a monetary standpoint; but in terms of leaving responsible and God fearing adults, we have great hope for their future. May God bless your family as well as ours as we strive to do His will.

In Him,
Don and Linda Torode

Chapter 49

10 Tips To Prevent
Parenting Burnout

1. Use Your Time Wisely.

As parents we have many schedules and time demands, not only on our work schedules but our parenting schedules as well. If both parents are working, which is usually the case, you may have to set aside family times days in advance and decide not to let anything interfere. Your family is more important than anything. Yes, jobs are important but keep in mind that you only have your teens for a short period of time and you need to make the most of it.

2. Do Not Over Volunteer Yourself.

If you are so involved with outside activities that you do not have as much time for your family you have over extended yourself. You can even over volunteer yourself at church. Yes, this sounds strange, but I do not think that God wants you so busy that you do not have time for your family. Problem: After you do all you can at church, school, or other civic organizations, you are so burned out that you do not have anything left for your teen.

3. Share Your Load.

Parenting is an awesome responsibility and should be shared by both spouses. It is not right for one person to have all of the responsibilities of raising a family while another person gives directions from a recliner with a remote in their hands. Much burnout is caused by being over worked whether it is on an outside job or the responsibility of parenting.

4. Take Short Breaks.

You may have to take a walk down the street or a ride across town but you need to take a few short breaks as much as possible. A short battery charge never hurt anyone. Finding short breaks after your children get to be teens is not as hard as when they are younger because you do not have to have a sitter to stay with them. You may not think you need to get away but it always helps when you do.

5. Make Time For Yourself Weekly.

This is different from taking a short break, this is actually having a planned activity. It may just be for an hour one day a week or it may be a college class. To what extent you do this will be determined by your burnout needs. Again, do not get so involved that you burnout on your activity and take it out on your family. Use balance.

6. Face One Problem At A Time.

Most people become frustrated and burned out when they try to handle multiple problems at once. Just about the time you get one problem solved another one is waiting in the wings. May a list of your problems, prioritize the list, and begin to solve them as quickly as possible. As soon as you get one finished mark it off and move on to the next one. Use this method whenever possible.

7. Share Your Thoughts With A Friend.

There is nothing like having a friend to share your thoughts, concerns, and victories with. Try to find a friend who has experienced many of the same burnout symptoms that you have. Find someone who has overcome the "parenting teen" years and seems to have been successful. Ask them how they handled burnout or other frustrations caused by parenting. Also, try to find someone that you can minister to who has a similar problem. You always learn more and feel better by helping others.

8. Expect Help From Your Spouse.

Do not just casually hint to your spouse that you need help, but let them know that you expect them to help. It is not even close to being fair for one person to get stuck with all of the work. There is absolutely nothing wrong with a husband washing clothes, cleaning bathrooms, vacuuming the house, or cooking supper, just to name a few ways he can help. Many husbands already do those things and for those we say a hearty "thank you." Now, you go find your wife and thank her for all she does.

9. Reward Yourself.

I really like this suggestion. Give yourself a reward each month for successful parenting. You and your spouse may set aside one night a month to go out to eat just to reward yourself for parenting as hard as you can. You may go out for other reasons, but this should be a tradition because of your parenting. Of course there are other ways to reward yourself such as buying yourself a gift. Whatever works best for you, do it.

10. Do Not Be Afraid To Ask For Help.

There may be a time when you have to ask for outside help. This help would come from someone other than your family or a close friend. This person may be a counselor or minister type person. It is definitely not a slap in your face to ask for help. If you had a broken arm you would most certainly get it fixed. The same is true with fixing emotional problems as well.

Dear Parents,

My wife and I have been married for 25+ years, and are the parents of two boys, Christopher, age 22, and Benjamin, age 10. Let me say right here and now that we are by no means experts at parenting.

However, Deborah and I have learned some lessons through the years that might be of interest to you as you parent your children. We hope these lessons are beneficial in helping you avoid parenting burnout in the years to come.

First, please do not lose your identity to your children. You do not cease to exist when your children are born. Instead of becoming little Susie's father, or little Johnny's mother, why not allow them to be know as Mrs. So and So's Child? Don't become so wrapped up in your children that you cease to be.

Second, to avoid burnout, step out. Your children need the break, whether you do or not. Get away from the children. If you can do it on a regular basis, great! If you can't, do it as often as possible. Nothing will burn you out quicker as a parent that being with those little angels 24-7.

Third, please, don't take this parenting thing too serious. Yes, I know, it is serious business, but, folks, it is fun business also. Enjoy it! Have a blast! Learn to laugh at yourself. Know when to hug'em and when not to hug'um. Don't be afraid of making mistakes or asking for forgiveness. You'll enjoy it a lot more.

Finally, to avoid parenting burnout, partner with God. He hasn't burned out yet, and He's been doing this a lot longer than you and I. Make His Word your daily companion. Make prayer your daily practice. Let Him lead you as you lead your children.

> In His Love,
> Rodney & Deborah Tidwell

Chapter 50

10 MORE Virtues To Instill In Your Teen

1. Hospitality.

Hospitality is the practice of entertaining friends or strangers with kindness and liberality. "Keep on loving each other as brothers. Do not forget to entertain strangers, for by so doing some people have entertained angels without knowing it" (Hebrews 13:1-2). "If there is a poor man among your brothers in any of the towns of the land that the Lord your God is giving you, do not be hardhearted or tightfisted toward your poor brother. Rather be open-handed and freely lend him whatever he needs" (Deuteronomy 15:7-8).

2. Gratitude.

Gratitude is the state of being thankful; appreciation of favors received; response to kindness. "Always giving thanks to God the Father for everything, in the name of our Lord Jesus Christ" (Ephesians 5:20). "Be joyful always; pray continually; give thanks in all circumstances, for this is God's will for you in Christ Jesus" (I Thessalonians 5:16-18).

3. Courtesy.

Courtesy is politeness combined with kindness; it is con-sideration for the feelings of others. "Finally, all of you, live in harmony with one another; be sympathetic, love as brothers, be compassionate and humble. Do not repay evil with evil or insult with insult, but with blessing, because to this you were called so that you may inherit a blessing" (I Peter 3:8-9). "Suppose a man comes into your meeting wearing a gold ring and fine clothes, and a poor man in shabby clothes also comes in. If you show special attention to the man wearing fine clothes and say, ' Here's a good seat for you, 'but say to the poor man, 'You stand there, 'Or, Sit on the floor by my feet,' have you not discriminated among yourselves and become judges with evil thoughts?" (James 2:2-4).

4. Punctuality.

Punctuality is the quality of being prompt, especially in keeping an appointment or engagement; of observing, or doing, at the precise and exact time. "There is a time for everything, and a season for every activity under heaven" (Ecclesiastes 3:1).

5. Ambition.

Ambition is the desire a person may have to achieve a certain goal, or to obtain some object. "Lazy hands make a man poor, but diligent hands bring wealth. He who gathers crops in summer is a wise son, but he who sleeps during harvest is a disgraceful son" (Proverbs 10:4-5). "We hear that some among you are idle. They are not busy; they are busybodies. Such people we command and urge in the Lord Jesus Christ, to settle down and earn the bread they eat. And as for you, brothers, never tire of doing what is right" (2 Thessalonians 3:11-3).

6. Loyalty.

Loyalty may be defined as faithfulness to country, friend, promise, or duty; fidelity. "Dear friend, you are faithful (loyal) in what you are doing for the brothers, even though they are strangers to you" (3 John 5). "So then, men ought to regard us as servants of Christ and as those entrusted with the secret things of God. Now it is required that those who have been given a trust must prove faithful (loyal)" (I Corinthians 4:1-2).

7. Reliability.

Reliability is the state or quality of meriting trust or confidence; trustworthiness; dependability. "Whoever can be trusted with very little can also be trusted with much, and whoever is dishonest with very little will also be dishonest with much. So if you have not been trustworthy in handling worldly wealth, who will trust you with true riches? And if you have not been trustworthy with someone else's property, who will give you property of your own?" (Luke 16:10-12).

8. Self-Reliance.

Self-reliance is defined as reliance on, or confidence in, one's own ability, efforts, or judgment. "Each one should test his own actions. Then he can take pride in himself, without comparing himself to somebody else, for each one should carry his own load" (Galatians 6:4-5). "And we know that in all things God works for the good of those who love him, who have been called according to His purpose" (Romans 8:28).

9. Discernment.

Discernment is clearness in judgment; penetration; insight; the power of distinguishing; faculty of nice or exact judgment. "So give your servant a discerning heart to govern your people and to distinguish between right and wrong. For who is able to govern this great people of yours? The Lord was pleased that Solomon had asked for this. So God said to him, 'Since you have asked for this and not for long life or wealth for yourself, nor have asked for the death of your enemies but for discernment in administering justice, I will do what you have asked. I will give you a wise and discerning heart, so that there will never have been anyone like you, nor will there ever be" (I Kings 3:9-11).

10. Foresight.

Foresight is the power or act of seeing in advance; heedful, thought for the future; prudence; prevision, forethought, or care. "A prudent man sees danger and takes refuge, but the simple keep going and suffer for it" (Proverbs 22:3). "Why, you do not even know what will happen tomorrow. What is your life? You are a mist that appears for a little while and then vanishes" (James 4:14).

Dear Parents,

The greatest virtue that a teen or anyone else could have is really not hard to determine. It is not a new concept or a new revelation to mankind. It is that of love.

When I think of the people that have touched my life such as Granny Hale or my Aunt Lucille, I am reminded of their love for everyone. No matter who they came in contact with they always had an encouraging word and a smile. There was never a question if these ladies possessed the Spirit of God. The love of that only comes from God, which was embedded deep in their soul.

In the movie "The Sound of Music", the governess Maria sings a song of encouragement of what to do when you are having a bad day. "When the Bee Stings—When the Dog Bites." Maria tells us to think of good things, "Brown paper packages tied up with strings". Well, I think of the strong Christian love that Granny Hale and Aunt Lucille have for me.

The Apostle Paul inspired from God tells us in II Corinthians 13 the greatest virtue we can have is that of love. What influence we can have when we really live the love of God. Without thinking we live the life of a servant, just like our Lord and Savior Jesus Christ. When we have the love of God in our hearts every other virtue falls into place. There's no question of honesty or work ethics. All of the ingredients necessary for sound moral character come naturally when you have and live the love of God. Diligently teach your teen love, honesty, and a strong work ethic and they will go far.

In Love,
Johnny & Lindy Blanchard

Chapter 51

10 Questions Parents Need To Constantly Ask Themselves About Parenting

1. Am I Doing All I Can Possibly Do To Get My Family To Heaven?

John Maxwell says, "I am responsible to you, not for you." We cannot force our kids to follow God, but we can provide every resource and instruction needed for them to make their own decisions.

Find a quiet spot and list at least five ways that you are now using to get your family to heaven. Write them on paper so you will be able to see them often. Once a week pull out the sheet to remind yourself of the priority of God in your home.

2. Do I Really Have A Balanced Lifestyle?

Is my lifestyle balanced in such a way that my family has quality and quantity time? Do I keep things such as sports, shopping, or other activities in the proper place in my life? Is my home-life centered around Sports Center or soap operas?

Probing questions about balance allow us to discover what we are filling our lives with. For the next two weeks keep an activity journal. Write down everything you do. At the end of the two weeks you will know how much and what kind of television you watch. You will know how often your family eats together. All of this will provide the tools needed to evaluate and balance your household's lifestyle.

3. Am I Being A True Witness For Jesus?

Our teens will be able to see our spirituality as well as hear us talk about it. Do we walk the walk as much as we talk the talk in our witness for Jesus? Do we have people in our home, teach a class, or study and pray on a regular schedule? Do our teens see us involved in witnessing?

4. Am I Teaching My Family What They Need To Survive In This World?

"Survive" is a true term for today's society. More than ever our children need to know how to, as Harvey McCay puts it, swim with the sharks without getting eaten alive.

What am I teaching my teens at this point to help them survive in this world? What am I teaching my teens to help them get ready to leave home for college or the business world? List several ways in which you are doing the above and place them where you can be reminded of them daily.

5. Do I Challenge My Teen Appropriately?

Often we as parents, and especially dads, challenge our teens to do their best in sports. However, are we challenging them in other areas of their lives? Do we challenge them to be all they can be in their faith? Do we challenge them to take part in community projects that benefit others?

Challenge with reward. Let's praise our kids when they accept and meet the challenge. Instead of acting like we expected it and the reward is the accomplishment, we need to verbally encourage them to let them know how proud we are of them.

6. Am I An Encourager?

Do I encourage my teen in all areas of his/her life? Do I allow them to fail and then to do better the next time? Praising is also a way of disciplining your teen. Usually when we think of discipline we think of it in a negative way such as being put on restriction or having their car taken away for the weekend. It is highly possible that your teen will do better because you are a great encourager.

7. Do I Allow My Family To Become Involved In Watching And Listening To Negative Media?

We do not have to be told many times how bad television, movies, and music can be on our teens if used in a negative way. How many murders do they see a year on television? How many sex scenes do they see on television and at the movies in a year's time? Have you listened to the words of their newest CD? Take time to preview what they are watching and listening to through the media.

At the risk of sounding over the top, unchecked media is an invitation for Satan to infiltrate our hearts. His key is making media so subtle, and so innocent. As long as we are watching it and not doing it we feel justified. Yet, God calls us to holiness not just in our action, but in our lifestyle.

8. Am I Spoiling My Teen?

I cannot tell you how many spoiled teens I have dealt with in the last thirty years. On one particular occasion I recall a teen being promised a Harley Davidson motorcycle if he would go before the church and rededicate his life. Within a week he went before the church and two weeks later he had a candy apple red motorcycle. I know this is an extreme example, but we spoil them in other ways. Try to think of the ways that you may be guilty of spoiling your teen and pray that God will show you the ways to be good to your children without spoiling them.

9. How Often Do I Say, "I Love You?"

Does your teen constantly hear "I love you?" Is this something you say to them daily? If you don't already, pick a time and tell them how you really feel about them. Be honest and sincere about your feelings and never let them doubt that you love them unconditionally.

Don't get concerned about the brush-off, or lack of interest by your teen. If your family openly loves it may be they have grown used to the words. If your family rarely displays affection for each other, they may be so shocked they do not know the proper reaction.

10. What Else Can I Do For My Teen?

This seems like a small question to be asking yourself, but it is really a huge one. Think of other ways you can help your teens. Do you need to spend more time with them or communicate more? Do you need to be a better encourager or disciplinarian? Think of ways to help, jot them down, and go for it.

Dear Parents,

Ever second-guessed yourself? Ever wondered if the advice, or punishment, or reward for your teen(s) was right? Have you ever wished you could do some part of your relationship with your teen(s) over? Have you ever wondered why you even had children to begin with? Welcome to the show. You get to spin again. Most parents of teens ask these same questions that you and I are asking. Let us add one more question to your list. Are you asking the right questions? Are you asking questions that concern not only the social and emotional welfare of your teen(s), but the spiritual welfare as well?

In America, we get caught up in trying to provide our teen(s) with everything they want. We are concerned about how they fit in at school and what they are wearing. Research shows that parents of teens are almost possessed with their teen(s) making good grades, above all else. They have more disposable income than any other generation ever, and there still seems to be something missing-- something they can't buy.

We are right in the middle of rearing a teenage son and a pre-teen son. We used to have all the answers to all the questions about teens. Now we read and pray a lot. We spend a lot of time trying to make sure our boys are around significant other people--and teens. We are reading all those books about teens that we used to give parents in our youth group. We are looking for answers to the old and the new questions.

This chapter deals with some of the questions that are most important in the lives of our children and families. They touch on the spiritual side and, after all, what is really important for our teen(s)? As you read and study through this chapter, we pray that you will be encouraged and enlightened. We think you will be challenged, and hopefully, you will put some of the suggestions into practice.

> Don't Give Up,
> Dudley and Vicki Chancey
> Director of Youth Ministry
> Oklahoma Christian University

Chapter 52

10 Tips for Assigning Chores at Home

1. Assign Or Agree On Chores.
    This will give you an opportunity to communicate with your teen. As a parent you should tell him/her or agree on the chores that need to be done. You might list five chores and let him/her choose three to do. You might just assign the chores that you feel need to be done. Make the ramifications clear if the chores are not done and done right. Also, reward them for a job well done even if it's a pat on the back or a word of encouragement.

2. Do Not Stand Over Your Teen.
    Once the chores have been assigned or agreed upon allow your teens to do them without you standing over them. Allow them to do them well or to fail. More lessons are learned from failure than success.

3. Encourage Them To Do It Right The First Time.
    Teach them the concept of doing things right the first time. It usually takes less time to do it right than having to go back and do it over again. Explain that they are going to have to do the chores right so they might as well do it right from the start. Does all of this seem like an echo from your parents in years gone by?

4. Clarify The Rules For Doing The Chores.
    Make it clear that if the chores are not done to your satisfaction that there will be discipline administered. I am not necessarily talking about physical discipline but discipline which will help them learn to do the chores right. You may take away the phone for a week or cut down on their television time. Whatever you decide, be consistent and be loving.

5. Know The Rewards.

Just as you are rewarded with your paycheck for doing a good job at your place of employment your teen wants to be rewarded as well for doing a good job on his/her chores. It is usually good for them to know the rewards before the chores are started, and it might give them an initiative to do better.

6. Use A Timetable.

After the chores have been agreed upon or assigned set up a schedule for the chores to be complete. If mowing the lawn is one of the chores, put a timetable on that chore. If not, you might come home two weeks after telling your teen to mow the lawn and it still not be done. You might hear, "You didn't tell me I had to mow it this month."

7. Allow No Complaining While They Work.

I'm sure you have heard the phrase, "whistle while you work." That simply means enjoy what you are doing while you are doing it. The point is - you are going to have to do the work so why not enjoy it or at least make it bearable? Going into a chore in the right frame of mind is "key" for teens and adults.

8. Do Not Expect Your Teen To Do Chores Just Like You Do.

When it is time to vacuum you may start at one point in the back bedroom and move to the front of the house. Your teen may want to start in the front of the house and move to the back bedroom. In most situations it really doesn't matter how it is done just so it is done and done right. Let them choose their way of doing things if it doesn't matter.

9. Work On Patience.

This is usually a "biggie" for most parents. We have been doing things for so long and doing them the way we want them done that we think it is the only way or the only time. We may, for years, get up on Saturday morning, vacuum the house, clean the bathrooms, and scrub the kitchen floor. Have patience if your teen wants to do it on Saturday afternoon or some other appropriate time.

10. Show Appreciation And Encouragement For A Job Well Done.

Our society seems to have become a negative society. We will really get onto a teen if they do not do a job well, but, if they do it well many times we will just shrug it off as something they are expected to do. Give them ample praise for a job well done.

Dear Parents,

While trying to teach our teenagers to work we made a lot of mistakes but let's not talk about those. There are few ways that come to mind that really helped as we taught the concept of working.

First, start early. There used to be a little story circulating about a mother of a three year old who asked the minister when she would start bringing her child to Sunday School. The minister replied, "Madam, you're already three years late." If you wait until your child is a teenager before requiring them to work, it will be very difficult, and you're already about ten years late.

Young children (as a rule) like to do chores and they like to please their parents. As they get older this becomes less true, but hopefully they set the pattern. As they do their chores at home, talk to them about when they get older they can go out and get a job and make their own money. I have a friend that told me years ago: Tell your child over and over and over what you expect of them. We don't think they are listening and they don't want us to know they are listening, but they are—and we found this to be true. It is our responsibility to tell them.

Second, be an example. We came from a large family that worked. We were expected to work and we did. Don't guess we ever thought about not working. In turn, we expected ours to work, and they did. Maybe they were embarrassed to sit around and do nothing while we worked. Somewhere along about this time you may become a "mean mama." Be patient! In a few years, especially after they become parents, they will "marvel" that you survived with your sanity. Of course, ours wonder about my sanity to this day.

Third, do what's best for that child not what's easier for you. It would be easier to do the chores in half the time and let them play. It takes time to check and see that the chores are done or insist that they go back and do them over. It would be easier just to give them everything they wanted than insist they get out and get a job. But what is best for the child? Having a job, earning money and being responsible for managing that money is what makes them responsible adults. Young people want vehicles and we learned they take better care of one they buy with money they worked for and usually drive more carefully if they pay for insurance.

We've always believed that if you will work, you can find a job. It is said that Tom Estes used to ask people that applied for a job at his place. "Do you want a job or do you want to work?" Even if that job is not what you want, if you will give it your best, something better will come along.

I read a little quote recently, "Truth is so rare these days, and it's a delight to hear it. I don't know how rare hard working teenagers are these days, but it's always a delight to hear about them."

Those teens will soon be husbands, fathers, wives and mothers. We want our in-laws to like us, don't we? The man with one talent who did nothing was called wicked and lazy, and the talent he had was taken away. If we do everything we can and fail, we tried. If we do nothing and fail, we live with regrets.

> Keep Working,
> Bill & Joe Ann Norris

Chapter 53

10 Things Teens Should Know About Life

1. "The World Owes You Nothing."

I had a friend who was always upset because he didn't win the lottery. Even though he never bought a ticket he always felt like he should win. He felt as though someone should walk up to him and just hand him 8 or 10 million dollars.

2. "Developing A Great Self-Image Is Up To You."

Parents can furnish all of the necessary ingredients to help their teen develop a positive self-image but it is ultimately up to them to make it happen. All the books, videos, and self-help tapes can be purchased for your teen's self-improvement, but if they are not willing to pay the price to make it happen you may be in for a disappointment as a parent.

3. "Don't Blame Others For Your Mistakes."

One parent puts it well, "When you, as a teen, make a mistake you need to accept the responsibility. Never try to put the blame on others when you are the one at fault. If you didn't pass a test don't blame it on the teacher who didn't explain things well. You might want to think back on the amount of time you studied or procrastinated getting prepared for the test. At any rate, accept the fact that you were unprepared."

4. "Never Make Excuses."

Making excuses is just another way of blaming others or trying to hide the fact that a teen didn't do what he was supposed to do. Rationalizing and justifying are the first steps on the long road of irresponsibility. Explain to your children that a quick apology and ready acceptance of responsibility will lead to more opportunities and greater respect as an individual.

5. "Hard Work And Dedication Pay Off."

I have often heard it said, 'What if the person who invented WD40 had quit on WD39?' Hard work and dedication will go a long way to accomplishing what life has in store for you. There are those who will hire a hard working, dedicated person over someone who is well qualified in other areas.

6. "Face Your Problems Head-On."

If you are faced with a problem meet it head-on, get it solved, and move on. If you wait for problems to solve themselves many times they will only become worse. Face your problems with prayer, patience, and humility.

7. "Do Not Expect Everything To Be Handed To You."

If you want a good job, work for it. If you want good grades, work for them. If you want a great family life, put forth the effort to make it happen. Never sit back and wait for things to happen, get up and make things happen. Be in control of your situations and don't wait for someone to control them for you.

8. "No whining."

Mike Root says that he is astounded that people can go from singing "Amazing Grace" to Amazing Gripes so quickly. Whining will only make your teen look like a baby to others. Few firms will want a person on staff who constantly bellyaches and complains. By refusing to put up with a sour attitude you will be saving your child a lot of future embarrassment.

9. "Never Take Things For Granted."

There are many things in our lives that we take for granted. Many of these can be changed in a split second. One minute you may be really healthy and suddenly there is some type of illness or accident that takes that health away from you. You may have friends one minute and because of the way you treat them the next minute they may be gone. Don't even take life itself for granted; most everyone has been touched with the loss of a loved one. Not taking things for granted allows a person to live each moment for all its worth.

10. "Don't Sit Back, Get Up And Make Things Happen."

One of my favorite questions I ask when I pass a teen at church is "What's happening?" They usually reply by saying, "Nothing." My response to that is "Well, get up and make things happen. Don't wait for it to happen, make it happen." Don't go through life and look back on the things you could have done or the changes you could have made. Do it now before it's too late.

Dear Parents,

To begin with, let me say that even though I am a marriage and family therapist, even though we have two teens and one pre-teen, even though I have helped parents struggling with their kids for almost 20 years, even though my wife is an excellent mother--we do not have all the answers when it come to raising kids. We thought we did, then our kids turned into teenagers! We struggle just like all parents with teens. We pray daily for wisdom from God. We tell our teens, "Look, we are new at this parenting thing too! Let's be patient with each other." My wife and I often pray, "God, just don't let us brain damage our kids!"

There are several things we want our children to know before they leave home. They are: (1) Take the responsibility for your own actions. Don't blame others when things do not go the way you planned or you fail at something. Just pick yourself up and start over. (2) Do not just aimlessly stroll through life thinking that the world owes you a living. The world absolutely owes you nothing. If you want to make a good living you have to put your nose to the grindstone and make things happen. (3) You should always honor your spouse. As a therapist, I grow weary hearing couples say; "I just don't love my spouse anymore. I am just not happy." My professional response? "So what ! You probably don't feel like you are in love anymore because you are not behaving like you are in love anymore! If you continually honor and praise your spouse, your spouse will, in all probability, honor and praise you in the same way. In other words, make your spouse your best friend. (4) Never take your life's situations for granted. Be constantly in touch with God and thank Him for what He has supplied you with. Your health, finances, life-style, family, and your relationship with Him and His Church.

Yes, raising teens is a very tough job. However, raising teens is also a very rewarding time in the life of a parent. We see a few failures but we also see numerous successes. Let me encourage you to memorize Deuteronomy 6:6-9, "These commandments that I give you today are to be upon your hearts. Impress them on your children. Talk about them when you sit at home and when you walk along the road, when you lie down and when you get up. Tie them as symbols on your hands and bind them on your foreheads. Write them on the doorframe of your houses and on your gates."

> May God Bless You,
> Mitch & Rhonda Temple

Chapter 54

10 Tips Used To Slow Down
Family Conflict

1. Keep Conversation Levels Low And Positive.

I know this may be hard to believe but raising your voice by screaming and yelling only adds to the confusion. Parent/teen conflicts are usually a power struggle with each party trying to gain control of the conversation. Make your mind up before the conflict starts that you are going to be in control and you are going to do it with a low voice and sense of being positive. Pray about it before it happens and ask God for wisdom (James 1:5).

2. Listen Carefully.

We have already stated in another chapter that God gave us two ears and one mouth so we should listen twice as much as we talk. Listening takes patience for most people; to others it comes naturally. If you condition yourself to be a good listener you will have fewer opportunities to scream and yell like we discussed above. Listening is the most important part of communication.

3. Do Not Judge Motives.

Have you ever geared yourself up to face a problem and it turned out to be totally different than what you expected? Maybe your teen wanted to talk to you and you were ready to face a huge problem and it turned out to be nothing significant. Never judge their motives for asking something until you know for sure what the situation is. This is accomplished by your teens first earning your trust.

4. Do Not Lose Your Temper.

The second that you lose your temper during a conflict, the other party immediately gains control of the situation. Now the problem is not what you were discussing, it is your temper. After the discussion is over and you have settled down you finally realize that now there are two problems instead of one, the conflict and your temper. It will be very difficult to solve one without solving the other.

5. Ask Questions.

Asking questions is a necessity during a family conflict; the challenge is to ask them in the right way. Make your tone of voice pleasant and non-threatening. Ask questions to seek information, not to "push buttons."

6. Share Your Feelings.

Let your teens know how you feel. Again, do it in a non-threatening way as not to make the tension rise in the room between the two of you. By sharing your feelings it is possible that conflicts will be minimal. Example: You might explain to your teens why they can't go to a concert that they want to attend. Safety reasons, spiritual reasons, etc. Are they going to understand your reasoning? Probably not, but it might cut down on the level of conflict.

7. Maintain Eye Contact.

In most cases, if you maintain eye contact with your teens it will allow you to be in control. Most teens will look away or scan the room while you are talking. Eye contact is a form of control so use it. Try it sometimes when you are not in a conflict and see how it works for you.

8. Attack The Problem And Not The Person.

We make a huge mistake when we start out trying to solve a problem and end up attacking the person instead of the problem. We get in a conversation with our teens and our tone of voice gets higher and higher. The next thing you know we are in a verbal "war" with each other and nothing is being solved. Focus on the problem, solve it, and do not create new problems with your attacks.

9. Spend Time Together.

Cutting down on conflicts may be handled by just spending more time with each other. I feel that many times we don't even know each other as well as we should because we only spend time with each other when necessary.

Try to get closer to your teens, become their friends. Do I mean become their very best friend? Possible but not probable. Just be a friend.

10. Admit When You Are Wrong.

It is so difficult for most people to admit when they have made a mistake, especially to their teens. Maybe you made a decision about something that affected your teens and it was the wrong decision. Simply apologize and move on. This will teach them that it is okay to change their minds or that we as parents may be wrong sometimes.

Dear Parents,

We are writing this letter hoping to encourage you and your relationship with your children. We would like to mention a couple of tips to help avoid conflict with your kids. Always try to choose your battles. Is what your children did really worth fighting over? I know it's easy to jump the gun and light into your kids. Try to give your kids a chance to explain what and why it happened. If it's not important try to compromise and discuss the issue. Always let the child know who is in charge.

Be consistent with what you say. Talk the issue over with your spouse. Many times your spouse may help you see the circumstance from a different light. Is it really worth getting worked up over? I know in our family my husband is the calm one. I'm the one who gets upset quickly. Sit your child down and talk about it. You and your spouse should be on the same wavelength, especially in front of the children. Let the strongest one discuss the matter and the other back him up. Let your children know that you are there for them and love them no matter how large or how small the problem is. Pray with your child to ask for guidance on both parts. Take one problem at a time if possible. They seem to come a dime a dozen sometimes.

We have three children, two teenagers and an eight year old. All three have different personalities and we have to handle each child differently. Let you children know you and your spouse discuss everything together. My daughter once told me when a problem came about that she was going to tell her dad. She couldn't understand why parents need each other's support. As she has gotten a little older she has told me several times she appreciates the discipline, but not at the time it was administered.

Don't get me wrong; we still have conflicts, but we try to choose our battles wisely. Anytime two or more people are together there's bound to be differences in opinion. I hope this letter will help you in the future. The thing I have found most effective in our family is to pray for guidance everyday.

Joe and Jackie Miller

Chapter 55

10 Warning Signs of Violent Behavior In Your Teen

1. Low Self-esteem.

How teens think about themselves directly ties into the way they treat others. The lower the self-esteem the greater the chance of physical violence. Their lack of concern for their own life causes a lack of concern for the lives of others.

2. Poor Grades in School.

It is not the grades in particular that brings about aggression. It is the way they think others perceive them because of the grades. Being labeled "stupid," "retard," "special ed," and other descriptions will cause some teens to retaliate with force. They feel that brawn will teach those with brains a lesson.

3. Constantly Blaming Others.

The "It's not my fault!" syndrome becomes more than a passing mood for those who lash out physically. They believe that "everyone" is against them. Subconsciously they imagine an ongoing conspiracy to derail their lives.

4. Rebels Against Authority.

What teen doesn't rebel, right? This type of rebellion includes multiple visits to the principal, police arrests, and possibly resisting arrest. They want to live by a different set of rules and believe that the law only acts as a barrier to their desired lifestyle.

5. Can't Control Their Anger.

Everyone gets mad, but not everyone destroys property in the process. At a local "Christian" high school a teacher offended a student. That night he revved up his motorcycle and spun donuts in her yard until it looked like someone had used a backhoe. Lack of control of that magnitude is more than "he's just being a teenager." As with the other points in this list, seek professional assistance before the situation escalates.

6. Extremely Introverted.

Introverts who become violent usually do so in an explosive manner. Why? Their nature refuses to let them release their tension through communication and other natural methods. As they continue to allow comments, aggravations, etc. build up in their lives they strike out in a dangerous fashion. These are the kids who get the comments like, "We never knew anything was wrong. She seems so quiet and sweet. Sure, some people made fun of her, but is was no big deal."

This is not to say that an introverted teen has violent tendencies. As a parent take special care for your introverted teen to make sure there is an avenue of release.

7. Recent Rejections Or Trauma.

Three teens were arrested at a military academy for sodomy against another student. Do you think the student might want revenge? Do you think those three guys might be in danger if they are allowed back on campus? While a situation of that magnitude might be rare, it is the sort of trauma that can cause an otherwise ordinary kid to become violent.

8. Turns Away From Friends.

A few chapters ago we discussed how a change in friends could result in a change of attitude and behavior. Turning away from friends can be a sign of distancing. That means they may have had some type of altercation and want to provide distance to explain their rash behavior. Feeling friendless provides an excuse for one to hurt the people who have hurt him or her. This is yet another reason for us as parents to be intimately involved in the lives of our kids.

9. Watches And Listens To Violent Media.

Most teens like action movies and music that contains a message of rebellion. When the lyrics and ideas on film find their way into real life it is a warning sign. Such as a teen who has no previous interest in guns starts buying magazines about explosives or semi-automatic weapons. Or a young person who gets involved in a chat room or other online discussion forum that centers on violent activities.

10. Withdraws From Family.

Sometimes a teen will draw away and form a disassociation from the family. I'm not talking about being dropped off a block from school so their friends won't see you together. If connection existed previously, then withdrawal includes a new pattern of ignoring family members, becoming increasingly disrespectful, and refusing to be involved in any kind of family activity.

Dear Parents,

I can't tell you how many times I have felt guilty for the way things turned out at our house with our teen. I can't tell you how many times I saw changes in the attitude in my teen but let it pass because I thought it was a temporary stage that teens go through. As he began to rebel against us and his teachers and coaches at school we knew something was wrong. This action was totally out of character for him, actions that we had not seen before. After several altercations at school we decided that something had to be done. It seemed like the more we did the worse the situation became. Our son began to wear a clothing style that was totally foreign to him six months before. He began to hang around people who were constantly in trouble at home and school and he would constantly defend them. We prayed, we talked with others, we searched for answers. We finally realized, after months of searching, that his main behavior problem was caused by the music he was listening to. He was consumed by thoughts of rebellion and even suicide. Yes, he had other problems which caused him to turn to this lifestyle. His problems caused his grades to drop, change friends, and totally drop out of church activities.

What did we do as parents? We faced his problems with

him. We told him we would not allow Satan to control him. We would do whatever we had to do to get him back where he needed to be as a Christian, a son, and a person in society. We did not realize that his self-esteem was so low because of not being able to have a "steady" girl friend like his friends did. He is immature when it comes to relationships with girls; they are much more mature than he is at this stage in his life. He's a great person and we love him to death. I just wish we had spent more time with him, asked him more questions, and even snooped around in his room if necessary to find out his problem.

Our son is getting help from a local Christian counselor. The counselor is working him through several processes which, we believe, will put him on the road to recovery.

God is really working in our family. We have learned a lot as parents and our son has learned a lot as well. One thing we have learned is how to help other people who are in the same type situations.

Don't Give Up,
Dwayne & Diane Davis

Chapter 56

10 "Wants" Teens Want From Their Parents

1. Parents Who Are Spiritual Leaders.

It would be hard for me to number the times when teens have told me that they really want their parents to be strong spiritual leaders. However, they usually will not state this fact in front of their friends. As parents we should take every opportunity to teach them about Christ and His Church. Spend time with them daily sharing the blessings of God.

2. Parents Who Are Fair With Discipline.

Many times we as parents get "caught up in the moment" and are very unfair with our discipline tactics. At a time when everything is going great, sit down with your teen and talk about discipline. Decide together what the consequences will be if certain problems take place. Above all be consistent with your discipline. Do not put them on two weeks restriction one time and two days the next for the same offense. Also, teach them the positive effects of self-discipline.

3. Parents Who Are Easy To Talk With.

It is an awesome compliment for a parent to hear that their teen made the statement, "I can talk to my parents about anything." Teens want to be heard by their parents so it is very important that we develop great listening skills. It is also very important that we communicate with them in a calm voice. I can promise you that if you listen to them and talk with a gentle tone they will come back for more advice in the near future. Be gentle and listen.

4. Parents Who Are Open And Honest.

All throughout scripture we are taught the importance of honesty in the way we treat others. We are taught to love our neighbors as ourselves. We are taught to put others above ourselves. The same holds true with our teens. Be honest with them at all times. Let them know what is good for them and what is not. Also, be honest with them when you have made mistakes in parenting them. It is okay to be wrong but it is just as important to let your teen know that you were wrong and will do better next time.

5. Parents Who Respect Me.

One teen said, "I may not make the same decision as you do as parents, but my decision is not always wrong. If toilet paper comes off the top or the bottom, it really doesn't matter both ways are right." "Also, respect me for what I want to be and not what you want me to be. I want to play in the band and you want me to play football." Respect has to be earned, so give them the opportunity to do so.

6. Parents Who Show Appreciation For Me.

Can you imagine how a teen must feel when he or she is complimented by their parents, especially if praise is not a common practice in your home? Teens love to be bragged on by their parents. How would you feel if word got back to you that your teen was bragging on you around their friends at school? Maybe they were saying what great parents you are. Maybe they were bragging on how you treat them with love and respect. Well, they have those same feelings when you show appreciation for them.

7. Parents Who Spend Time With Me.

I have often heard it said that the way you spell love is TIME. You show your love by the amount of time you spend with your teens. Every minute counts so do not waste an opportunity to spend a few minutes each day with your teen. Even if you get in the car and ride around the block just to talk, do it. Let them know you care. Let them know you want to spend time with them. This is especially true in the early teen years. When they get a driver's license everything seems to change, so don't waste a moment.

8. Parents Who Welcome My Friends.

This is a very tricky subject. Oftentimes we see things in

their friends that they don't see. However, there are things they see in their friends that we do not. We may look at a friend's outward appearance and not like what we see. After we dig a little deeper we may find that this friend is a fine Christian teen. We also may find out that this friend is not such a great person and is a bad influence on your teen. It often hurts you and your teen to discuss friendships but we must do everything we can to save the soul of our child.

9. Parents Who Show Love And Appreciation for Each Other.

One of the greatest ways to teach a teen is by modeling. If we model a strong, loving, Christian relationship with each other, a great lesson has been taught. It is very difficult for us to tell our teens what kind of relationship to have with others if we do not do the same with each other. Let your teen see you holding hands, hugging, and yes even kissing occasionally. Let them hear you brag on each other. Make an opportunity to lift each other up, especially in front of your teens.

10. Parents Who Are Teaching Me To Be Independent.

I have heard it said many times, "Parent with the end in mind. Parent with the attitude that you are preparing them to leave the nest." This is great advice coming from a parent who has raised four godly children to adulthood. Do not be afraid to let them make a decision especially if they will learn from the outcome whether good or bad.

Dear Parents,

I would like to share something on my heart that hopefully will help in raising and dealing with your teens. Every teenager is an individual with a personality of his or her own. Allow your teens to make some difficult choices, instead of "laying down the law." I believe if parents could begin a democratic relationship with their teens from the beginning, then when situations arise, teens are less likely to feel threatened and alone. A democratic relationship is one in which the parent and teen are equally able to express feelings, opinions and talk about things with both sides respecting the other.

I also ask that you try to relate to your teens as best you can, and remember they are not a mirror image of you. I believe that Jesus Christ should be taught and discussed in the home, and that parents should take this role seriously. If teens are faced with temptations and the only basis they have for resisting is fear or the threat of a parent then under Satan's grasp they will not stand. It has been but a couple of years since I was in the same boat as some of your teens, and it's hard to live up to standards and expectations if they are unattainable.

Please remember that the standards are to be set by Jesus, who is forgiving, gracious and merciful. If you as parents set a godly example and are consistent with your spiritual responsibilities to your teens, they will see in you the love of God and respect you for it. In closing, remember Proverbs 22:6, "Train up a child in the way he should go: and when he is old, he will not depart from it."

In Christian Love,
Joy Millergren Smith

Chapter 57

10 Tips NOT To Do As Parents

1. Fail To Show Them Love.

There are many mistakes which may be made as a parent, but never make the mistake of failing to show your love for you teens. Demonstrating your love will cover a multitude of mistakes. Your teens will realize sooner or later that you have been sincere while trying to raise them to be the best they can be. This will especially hit home when they have children of their own.

2. Expect Them To Enjoy Your Hobbies.

This is especially tough for a daddy who loves sports and wants his son to play but the son has no real interest. He may be interested in the band or the school play and really want to be involved. Put your pride on the back burner and let him enjoy his hobbies. Like I said, this is tough.

3. Accept Less Than They Can Do.

They may struggle to make a "C" in school and that's okay if that is the best they can do but do not accept less. Most teens need to be encouraged and even pushed into making good grades or excelling in some activity. Let them try it on their own, but do not allow them to do less than they can do. Be an encourager, a motivator, or even a nag if need be. They may have to eventually fail at something in order for them to learn that they can succeed.

4. Force Them To Be What They Are Not.

Singing in the youth choir or youth group is very commendable but singing may not be their gift. Also, as bad as we hate to say it college is not for everyone either. This is extremely tough especially if Mom and Dad are college educated.

5. Fail To Discipline Them.

Proper discipline is key to the success of your teens. Remember, discipline is not always being negative like many may think. Praising your teens may also be used as discipline. You may praise a teen into making good grades or cleaning his room. Coaches praise their teams in the locker room before the big game to get them to excel on the field during the game.

6. Spoil Them.

Spoil them now and pay later. I have seen parents who give their teens everything and do everything for them. Later in life that teen does not cope so well when trying to accomplish a task. When they have to answer to a boss or someone in authority they may not be able to handle it without some type of altercation. Let them earn a few things. I promise, it will not hurt them.

7. Force Them To Play Sports.

You may encourage them to try sports to see if they like it, but do not force them to play. How would you feel if you forced them to play and they broke a leg or even their neck? If they do play sports let them play for fun and enjoyment and not for "blood and guts." I never thought I would be saying these things because I was a "blood and guts" dad when it came to sports.

8. Let Them Miss Church.

You are the parent and God put you in charge of making decisions until your teens are mature and able to make the proper choices. You may not believe it now but one day they will thank you for making them do things right, especially spiritual things.

9. Expect Perfection.

In all probability you will be very disappointed if you expect your teens to be perfect in every way. There is only one who is perfect and He is at the right hand of God. Think back on your teenage years; how perfect were you? I did not say that they should not do their best, but they will not be perfect in everything.

10. Be So Involved In Outside Activities That Your Teens Do Not Have Time For Family.

It is great for your teen to be involved in sports, band, school plays, church youth groups, or other activities but not to the extent of neglecting their families. List the activities, which they are involved in and how much family time they have. We only have them once, and for a short while, so let's make it count for God and family.

Dear Parents,

Our children are grown now. They are now out on their own—ages 30 and 25; it still sounds strange to hear myself say that. I suppose when they are little and at home, we just get so caught up in raising them that we forget they won't always be "little and at home." Actually, looking back, the few years we had to teach them how to live in this world went by with unbelievable speed.

Never say what your kids won't do. They may surprise you. Accept that even though they know how to act and what is and is not acceptable because you have taught them, there are many outside pressures that may cause them to do something totally different. No child is exempt from this fact. Do not excuse them for not doing what they should, but do understand that they are not perfect.

Do not talk negatively about them to someone else in their presence. When you do so, in that child's mind you have already taken away his incentive to be someone you can be proud of. He feels worthless. If he knows you believe in him, it will help him to believe in himself. Even on those harried days when you would like to send them off to Jupiter, remember that the way you represent him to others may very well be teaching him how to represent himself. You don't always have to brag on him, but don't cut him down in from of him.

Do not keep the reins too tight. The older a child gets, the more responsible he should be for himself and his own actions. As character is developed and trust is earned, we believe parents should "let go" a little more and a little more. By the time he is ready to go off to school or out on his own, the freedom won't be a new thing he is not accustomed to. He will have made some mistakes while he is at home and you still have the opportunity to give him guidance. He should always know that even though he has the freedom to make some of his own choices his parents are always right there in the background observing and ready to help if needed.

Don't make promises you don't intend to keep. In the area of discipline, if you tell them to "stop or else," make sure to honor the "or else." Those promises are just as important as any other. If a child knows your threats are empty words, why should he be sure of anything else you tell him?

Don't be afraid to discipline. It is for the child's good. However, NEVER discipline a child without telling him you love him.

Don't be their friend at the expense of being their parent. They will have many friends, but only two parents.

Don't try to live the life you wish you had through your children. They may not want to play football, be a cheerleader, play piano, etc. Forcing them to do these types of things or even to excel at them can damage their self-esteem for life. Respect their individuality. Support them in what they desire to do as long as it is wholesome. When they ask you to do things with them, make every effort to do it. Try not to tell them you can't. They won't always want you around.

Don't EVER, EVER, and EVER, use your children as an excuse to not do God's work. Your children are going to see and learn of God through you. Take them with you to make visits, go door-knocking, etc. Not only will they be gaining valuable experience, but they will also open doors you can't.

Don't worry. You probably won't make the mistakes your parents made with you. There are plenty more out there you can call your own.

Good Luck,
Alex and Cindy Jackson

Chapter 58

10 Things Your Teen Will Always Remember About You

1. The Time You Gave Them.

I will always remember the time my dad and mom gave me while I was growing up. I remember the ball games, camping trips, hunting and fishing trips, teaching my Sunday school class, teaching me in school, and just hanging out. They also took the time to teach me right from wrong, even though I didn't always listen. You cannot replace time. Set aside time each day, or at least every couple of days to spend quality time with your teen.

2. Sharing Jesus With Them.

My parents, as I have, made a lot of parenting mistakes while I was growing up. One mistake they did not make was teaching us the love of Christ. They talked of how we had been blessed when I really didn't think we had very much compared to my friends. Always be a Jesus model for your teens, it will not go unnoticed.

3. The Financial Sacrifices You Made.

Coming from a one-income family as a teen was not easy on my family. I remember overhearing them discussing our financial problems and how they were going to fix them. Do not brag about what you do for your teens, but begin to include them in on a few financial discussions. Especially situations that will allow them to see the sacrifices you make. You might want to gain their input on handling financial problems just to teach them.

4. How You Communicated With Them.

Are you a screamer or a yeller? Do you non-verbally show that you are not interested or that you are disgusted with the conversation? Are you a good listener? Practice being a good listener and answering in a calm, clear voice. Is it easy for most? No. Can it be done? Yes.

5. How You Disciplined Them.
I cannot remember the enjoyment of my mom or dad spanking me. I cannot even remember the pleasure I received from being put on restriction. However, looking back on my life as a teen and all of the discipline I received I can honestly say that it was for the good. Hint: Discipline now or pay dearly later.

6. The Way You Accepted Them.
It would have really disappointed my dad if I had not wanted to play sports. He was a coach and a great athlete in his own right. I do believe he would have accepted me whether I played or not. Accept them for what they enjoy not what you want them to enjoy. They may actually love carrying a bass drum instead of a football.

7. How You Treated Their Friends.
I know it sounds like I had the perfect parents-they were really close-but I didn't. They could tell if a person was good for me to hang around with or not. Many times they misjudged a person but most times they did not. Treat their friends with respect until they prove you wrong.

8. The Way You Encouraged Them.
Do you encourage them when they do the best they can or do you insist that they do better? I talk with teens all the time who wish their parents would just say a few kind words of encouragement to them. Write them an encouraging note or make that unexpected phone call to them just to tell them how much you appreciate them.

9. How Much Laughter Was In Your Home?
I have laughed so hard at something my mom or dad would do that was absolutely hilarious. I can remember my dad cooking grits and putting red or blue food coloring in them just to spice things up a little bit. I remember him acting like he pulled a nickel out of my ear so I would have money to spend. Create laughter and fun in your home; your teens will remember it for a lifetime.

260

10. How You Talked *About* Others.

Your teens will remember how you talked about others whether positively or negatively. They will remember whether you cut people down or built other people up. Remember, you are being heard so make it good. I still appreciate my mother so much because of the way she compliments her minister and song leader to us. I appreciate how much she loves her Sunday school teachers and her friends a church. I am so glad that I learned those things from her.

Extra: How You Talk *to* Others.

It is very vivid in my mind how my dad taught me to talk to others. He would say, "It doesn't matter if a person is older or younger than you, you say "yes sir or no sir, yes ma'am, or no ma'am" to them if they have earned your respect. You may not agree with them but you respect them. My parents also taught us to say "thank you" and "no thank you." They also taught us to say "please." Saying, "Please pass the bread" is the only way you get it at my house. We were taught to show respect and to be thankful at our house.

Dear Parents,

Throughout my childhood I have retained countless memories of time spent with my family. The most precious of those is the quality time spent with my parents. From my first steps to my first day of college, both of my parents have lovingly been there for me. I couldn't have been born to any two finer people. My mama and daddy are truly angels, and I have been extremely blessed to have them in my life.

It's funny how time flies and people grow; yet memories stay the same. Some say memories are just a part of life, but I consider them as a gift from God. The majority of my memories pertain to incidents that I have had with my parents. It was certainly hard to select only a few because every day is an adventure with my parents, but I can remember a few specifically.

I was in the fourth grade and it was my very first major

field trip. I was so excited to be going to the Davis Theatre to see my very first "real" play. My mother volunteered to be a driver for the trip, and that seemed to make me even more excited. Well, the day finally arrived and to my surprise my mother didn't show up on time. I was so upset, I couldn't believe she forgot about everything. Throughout the first half of the play all I could do was hold back my anger. Surprisingly, before I could openly express my feeling to the girl that was sitting beside me I saw my mom running down the aisle. Come to find out she was in a traffic accident on her way to the school, and was unable to get there on time. She was so apologetic, and being 9 years old, all I cared about was not getting embarrassed. I don't think I even said that I was glad she was all right; in fact I didn't say much of anything. It took me 6 or 7 years to fully understand what she did for me that day. She could have easily gone home after the accident or called in to say she couldn't make it, but no, she came running just as fast as she could down that aisle keeping the promise she had made to her daughter. I never will fully understand a mother's love until I have a child someday, but I know that I have experienced it to its fullest. A mother sacrifices it all and, amazingly, then some.

Call it crazy, but the most memorable experiences with my daddy consist of a birdie, racket, and an extremely long net. Each summer day around sundown the biggest badminton tournament in the south took place, and it was in my backyard. The two greatest players step up to compete in the fiercest battle; actually it's just my daddy and me, but we like to boost up our egos a little bit. Last count we had reached over a hundred hits, the goal that had conquered, and the trophy was ours. Actually, in real life the goal was reached, the quality time spent playing badminton with my daddy will always be my trophy. All I can say now is "We are the Champions..."

Thanks Mom and Dad,
Heidi Brooks

Chapter 59

10 Tips To Stay Close To Your Child After The Teen Years

1. Continue To Give Your Family Top Priority.

Even after they have graduated, gone to college, sought a career, joined the military, or gotten married continue to keep them at the top of your priority list of concerns. Keep them at the top of your prayer list and continue to let them know that you love them unconditionally.

2. Face Problems Together As A Family.

Just because teens are grown and gone does not keep families from having problems. Your teen may have a problem when he/she gets to college or gets married which will need your assistance. Let them solve what they can, but be willing to help or support.

3. Build On Traditions And Great Memories.

It's great when your children come back home and start talking about the great times they had while living there. I love it when they get the photo album down just to reminisce. Continue to build traditions even after they are gone, it will pay off later.

4. Become Close Friends.

Many times after your teen has gone you become close friends. The pressure is off for you to have to discipline them all the time or know their every move. When they really begin to make their own decisions a great friendship may begin.

5. Celebrate Their Maturity.

Talk with them about their maturity. Let them know that you are proud of them, if you are, and the way they have turned out. It doesn't hurt to let them know that it was a struggle for you to get them where they are, but the time and effort was well worth it.

6. Let Them Make Mistakes.
They may still live at home after the teen years or they may have moved out. Whatever the case let them make their decisions and deal with whatever happens. Be available for advice but step back and let them go.

7. Get Involved In Their New Stage In Life.
During their teen years they may have been heavily involved in sports, band, or other school activities. When they leave the teen years they may become more involved in an occupation or marriage. Accept them where they are and enjoy them while you can.

8. Stay In Touch On A Regular Basis.
Stay in touch but don't get in their way. Many times right after a teen leaves home they will not be around very much. You will even get the impression that they don't care about you anymore. Give them time to find themselves in their new world and they will usually return with open arms.

9. Let Them Enjoy Their Friends And/Or Spouse.
If you are like a lot of parents you will feel left out when your teen leaves home and develops new friendships or gets married. As difficult as it may be, step back and let them enjoy their newfound acquaintances.

10. Love Them Unconditionally, Warts And All.
They may do things that we do not agree with when they leave but we have to continue to love them anyway. We have to be that safe haven for them when they need to return. They need to know that we care and that we are there for them if they need us. It has been said many times, "They will not know how we feel until they have children of their own."

Dear Parents,

While your children usually have no doubt about your love for them, perhaps what they want most from you as a parent as they "leave the nest" is your respect. This is manifested in several ways, which have helped us to keep a very close relationship with our daughters. First, respect them as full-fledged adults, just as you would any other adult person. Their privacy is a good place to start. While we are always interested in who their friends are, how their careers are progressing, how they are faring financially, etc., we try to remember that these are very personal areas of their lives. As parents, we want to always be available to lend a helping hand, give out advice, or just be there to listen. However, we try not to jump in and "solve" every problem or situation that arises. This is especially true if your child is married. As a parent, we must accept that some of our functions have been taken over by the new spouse. Embrace that new son or daughter-in-law as your own, and you will reap a double reward of having someone new to love as well as drawing your own child closer to you. You must also recognize that your children's friends may know more about the adult your child has become than you do.

Another factor in relating to our adult children has been our asking THEIR advice on a number of issues. Just because they are our children does not mean we cannot learn from them. Many times our children have been of great help to us in solving problems because of businesses and friends with which they were familiar. When you need their help in any way, don't be afraid to ask. Instead of viewing you as weak, they will love you for recognizing their abilities.

Still another way to stay close is to simply spend time with them. Try to plan family events around their schedules, if possible. Having Sunday dinner together as a family has been a very enjoyable tradition at our house. A part of planning social functions is realizing that our adult children are simply not going to be available for every invitation you offer. Just be glad for your times together, and they will want to be with you whenever they can.

Sincerely,
Pat and Deb Watkins

Chapter 60

10 Tips To Know If You Are Becoming A Successful Parent

1. Your Teen Takes Your Advice.

What a great feeling it is the first time your teen walks up to you and says, "I need your advice on something." You really feel like they trust your opinion and you know that something you have done or said over the years is finally sinking in. There may be a time when you need to ask for their advice on an issue. Teens usually do not seek the advice of their parents, so know that you are the exception and be glad.

2. Your Teen Talks With You.

Have you ever been just sitting around, watching TV, cooking supper, or just relaxing, and your teen walks up and starts a conversation? It may start like, "Hey Dad, how are you doing?" or, "Hey Mom, what's going on?" At any rate, you have absolutely done something right if your teen just wants to small talk with you for a few moments. One of the major problems in a parent/teen relationship is that the teens usually do not want to talk. Consider yourself blessed if they enjoy conversing with you.

3. You Have Fun Being With Each Other.

I remember the days when my son and I went fishing, hunting, and camping. We often reminisce about those days. I remember when my daughter would ask me to go out in the yard and shoot basketball, where she would let me beat her in a game of "horse." Does having fun with each other mean you are going to have problem-free parenting? Absolutely not, but it does let you know that you have done something right and the doors will be left open for you to enter their world.

4. Your Teen Listens To You.

When they ask for your advice is one thing, but when they listen to your advice, which they did not ask for that, is something else. If your teen listens to you, you have obviously given good advice to them while they were younger. I am not saying that they take your advice; I am simply saying that great things are happening with you and your teen when they listen to what you have to say. You obviously did a great job of listening to them because of the way they listen to you.

5. Your Teen Brings His/Her Friends Home.

If your teens are not ashamed to bring their friends home with them you have obviously done something right. I do not know of many, if any, teens that want their friends in their home if they know they are going to be embarrassed by their parents. I remember when my parents might not have thought that my friends were the best influence on me but they never embarrassed them or us by their actions.

6. Your Teen Confides In You About His/Her Problems.

I do not know of many greater compliments greater than your teen confiding in you when they have a problem. Usually they go to a close friend for someone who will not be judgmental or too opinionated. Consider yourself fortunate when your teen comes to you. Consider yourself blessed by your previous actions, which has caused your teen to trust you with their problems. Get on your knees right now and thank God, you are truly a blessed parent.

7. You Make Up Relatively Soon After Arguments.

Are arguments going to happen in families? Of course they are. Do they have to "fester" on for two or three days before someone finally says, "I'm sorry?" Of course they don't. You know you have done something right in your parenting adventure when your teen says, "I'm sorry, it was my fault. Can't we just work this out and move on?" Making up soon after arguments is a sign of a healthy environment.

8. You Have A Friendship Relationship.

I will never forget the relationship that I enjoyed with my mom and dad. My dad and I did so many things together such as hunting, fishing, camping, playing sports, and just "hanging out." I have three younger sisters so that took up most of Mama's time but we were just as close as my dad and I. My dad passed away several years ago, but I considered him not only my dad but one of my closest friends.

9. They Hurt When You Hurt And They Laugh When You Laugh.

As parents we hurt when they hurt and we laugh when they laugh. But maturity is setting in when they feel the same way about us as parents. I can remember our children being upset when we were upset and being happy when we were happy. It made me feel good that they had genuine feelings us. Now that they are married and gone I know even more that their concern for us is real. I know that they are concerned about our well being more than ever.

10. They Love You Unconditionally As You Do Them.

As a parent I made many, many mistakes while helping my wife raise our teens. I made many mistakes that I wish I could go back and change. I have apologized to my grown children for those mistakes and they have assured me that everything is okay and they love me no matter what. Love covers up a multitude of mistakes. I have made a lot of mistakes, but I have a lot of love for my children and they know it, that's why they love me unconditionally. I thank God for His unconditional love for me and for teaching me what unconditional love really is.

Dear Parents,

We would like to say from the beginning that we are not perfect parents, our four children are not perfect, nor our grandchildren. We will say, however, that we serve a perfect

God.

How is it that we raised four children who are all today adult, faithful working warriors in God's army? We can't honestly give specific steps that we took during their years at home. We can say that we prayed a lot and taught them to pray, to have love and respect for God and others, and that we would attend all services, no question. As mother and dad we tried to live Christ-like lives before them and taught them to say "I love you" with sincerity and conviction. A habit, I'm proud to say, they all practice today.

May we offer the following suggestions:

1. Pray with them and for them, often.
2. Don't hesitate to say "I love you" to them at every opportunity.
3. Tell them that your home is their home and will be for the rest of our lives.
4. Always leave the door of communication wide open.

Whatever we did as parents that resulted in our children remaining true and faithful to God and His Kingdom, any and all praise and honor and glory goes to our Creator, God Almighty.

With all our hearts, thank you God!
Tommy & Jannett Weldon

Appendix A

Assessing Your Parenting

Parenting can be broken down into many areas. We have chosen five major areas for you to consider. Each area will have ten points for you to grade your own *strengths* or *weaknesses*. On the line provided put an "S" for *strength* and a "W" for *weaknesses*. We would encourage you to find ways to turn your *weaknesses* into *strengths* and we would also encourage you to continue working hard on your *strengths*. To finalize this exercise list your *weaknesses* on one sheet of paper and your *strengths* on another. You may want to use the *check-off* system when you have completed working on a particular area.

COMMUNICATION

_____ I am a really good listener.
_____ I make time for communication with my teen.
_____ I communicate well non-verbally.
_____ I do not interrupt when my teen is talking.
_____ I am open and honest in my communication.
_____ I never communicate to my teen that he/she is
        worthless.
_____ I communicate praise and appreciation to my
        teen/s
_____ I apologize when necessary; I may not always be
        right.
_____ I am calm and do not lose my temper while com-
        municating with my teen.
_____ I constantly communicate love for my teen.

DISCIPLINE

_____ I establish rules and they are understood by my
        teen.
_____ I continually learn from my past mistakes.
_____ I punish when I am in a calm frame of mind.
_____ I understand that punishment is not the only
        form of discipline.

_____ I ask for advice from other parents.
_____ I study parenting to better myself as a parent.
_____ I use _teachable moments_ to prepare my teen for future life situations.
_____ I discipline myself as well as my teen.
_____ I do not compromise the established rules.
_____ I show and tell my teen how much I love him/her.

RESOLVING CONFLICT

21. _____ I try hard to stop a conflict before it begins.
22. _____ I focus on the problem and not the teen.
23. _____ I listen carefully before I react.
24. _____ I keep communication at a low verbal level.
25. _____ I do not show my anger or frustration in an irrational way.
26. _____ I spend time talking to my teen before a conflict occurs.
27. _____ I make sure consequences are understood before a conflict begins.
28. _____ I ask a lot of questions from my teen.
29. _____ I allow my teen to express feelings in a rational way.
30. _____ I begin and end the conflict with a time of prayer.

DEVELOPING SPIRITUALLY

31. _____ I am a good spiritual role-model for my teen.
32. _____ I talk to my teen about God's grace.
33. _____ I talk to my teen about Jesus and His love for us.
34. _____ I give of my financial blessings and teach my teen to do so.
35. _____ I constantly share with my teen how we have been blessed.
36. _____ I pray with and for my teen.
37. _____ I am seen by my teen studying God's Word.
38. _____ I speak positively about church and church members.

39. _____ I know who my teen's friends are.
40. _____ I know what activities my teen is involved in.

TIME MANAGEMENT

41. _____ I make time for my teen.
42. _____ I create ways and reasons to spend time with my teen.
43. _____ I schedule my time in advance for my family.
44. _____ I spend quality and quantity time with my teen.
45. _____ I communicate to my teen how great it is to spend time with him/her.
46. _____ I never act frustrated because I have to spend time with my teen.
47. _____ I realize that if I do not spend time with them now they may not spend time with me later.
48. _____ I make an extra effort to make our time extra special.
49. _____ I will begin now to make up for lost time with my teen.
50. _____ I realize that God has given me my time and my teen to use for His glory.

Verses for parents to lean on:

John 13:34-35
"A new command I give you: Love one another. As I have loved you, so you must love one another. By this all men will know that you are my disciples, if you love one another."

Proverbs 5:1-2
My son, pay attention to my wisdom, listen well to my words of insight, that you may maintain discretion and your lips may preserve knowledge.

Ephesians 6:1-3
Children, obey your parents in the Lord, for this is right. "Honor your father and mother—which is the first commandment with promise—that it may go well with you and that you may enjoy long life on the earth."

Romans 12:10-12
Be devoted to one another in brotherly love. Honor one another above yourselves. Never be lacking in zeal, but keep your spiritual fervor, serving the Lord. Be joyful in hope, patient in affliction, faithful in prayer.

Proverbs 17:6
Children's children are a crown to the aged, and parents are the pride of their children.

Deuteronomy 6:6-9
These commandments that I give you today are to be upon your hearts. Impress them on our children. Talk about them when you sit at home and when you walk along the road, when you lie down and when you get up. Tie them as symbols on your hands and bind them on your foreheads. Write them on the doorframe of your houses and on your gates.

Proverbs 29:17
Discipline your son, and he will bring you peace; he will bring delight to your soul.

Proverbs 4:10-11
Listen, my son, accept what I say, and the years of your life will be many. I will guide you in the way of wisdom and lead you along straight paths.

Joshua 24:15
But if serving the Lord seems undesirable to you, then choose for yourselves this day who you will serve, whether the gods of your forefathers served beyond the River, or the gods of the Amorites, in whose land you are living. But as for me and my household, we will serve the Lord.

Proverbs 22:6
Train a child in the way he should go, and when he is old he will not turn from it.

Acts 16:31
They replied, "Believe in the Lord Jesus, and you will be saved—you and your household."

Exodus 20:12
"Honor your father and your mother, so that you may live long in the land the Lord your God is giving you."

Psalm 127:3-5
Sons are a heritage from the Lord, children a reward from Him. Like arrows in the hands of a warrior are sons born in one's youth. Blessed is the man whose quiver is full of them. They will not be put to shame when they contend with their enemies in the gate.

Proverbs 23:24-25
The father of a righteous man has great joy; he who has a wise son delights in him. May your father and mother be glad; may she who gave you birth rejoice!

Ephesians 4:2-3

Be completely humble and gentle; be patient, bearing with one another in love. Make every effort to keep the unity of the Spirit through the bond of peace.

Matthew 5:14-16

"You are the light of the world. A city on a hill cannot be hidden. Neither do people light a lamp and put it under a bowl. Instead they put it on its stand, and it gives light to everyone in the house. In the same way, let your light shine before men, that they may see your good deeds and praise your Father in heaven."

John 14:12-14

I tell you the truth, anyone who has faith in me will do what I have been doing. He will do even greater things than these, because I am going to the Father. And I will do whatever you ask in my name, so that the Son may bring glory to the Father. You may ask me for anything in my name, and I will do it.

John 3:16-18

"For God so loved the world that he gave his one and only Son, that whoever believes in him shall not perish but have eternal life. For God did not send his Son into the world to condemn the world, but to save the world through him. Whoever believes in him is not condemned, but who- ever does not believe stands condemned already because he has not believed in the name of God's one and only Son."

Philippians 4:13

I can do everything through him who gives me strength.

I John 5:3-5

This is love for God: to obey his commands. And his commands are not burdensome, for everyone born of God has overcome the world. This is the victory that has over- come the world, even our faith. Who is it that overcomes the world? Only he who believes that Jesus is the Son of God.

Galatians 5:22-23

But the fruit of the Spirit is love, joy, peace, patience, kindness, goodness, faithfulness, gentleness and self-control. Against such things there is no law.

Galatians 5:14

The entire law is summed up in a single command: "Love your neighbor as yourself."

Appendix C

How much do you know?
Answer the following questions in the spaces provided:

1. What is your teen's favorite color?

2. What is your teen's favorite food?

3. What is your teen's favorite television show?

4. What is your teen's favorite sport?

5. Who is your teen's favorite sports hero?

6. Who is your teen's favorite music group?

7. What is your teen's favorite song?

8. How many hours a week does your teen spend watching television or movies?

9. How many hours a week does your teen spend on the Internet?

10. Who is your teen's greatest role-model outside your family?

11. What is the greatest complaint your teen has about your family?

12. What does your teen like most about your family?

13. What does your teen like most about church?

14. What does your teen like least about church?

15. Who is your teen's favorite Bible character?

16. What is your teen's favorite Bible verse?

17. When and how often does your teen pray?

18. When is the last time you studied the Bible together as a family?

19. When is the last time you prayed together as a family? (not meals)

20. Who is your teen's favorite role-model at church?

What do you plan to do now?

Suggested Readings:

Dare to Discipline
Dr. James Dobson

Parenting With Scripture
Kara Durbin

Teens In Two Worlds
Mike Cope

Winning the Parenting War
David Clarke, Ph.D.

Hide or Seek
Dr. James Dobson

Raising Great Kids
McCloud & Townsend

Mothers & Daughters
Marie Chapian

*Understanding Your
Teenager*
Rice & Veerman

The Strong-Willed Child
Dr. James Dobson

Love Must Be Tough
Dr. James Dobson

The 10 Commandments of Dating
Ben Young & Dr. Samuel Adams

Preparing for Adolescence
Dr. James Dobson

*Bringing Up Kids Without
Tearing Them Down*
Kevin Leman

Parents & Teenagers
Youth for Christ

Relational Parenting
Ross Campbell, M.D.

Put It To The Biblical Test:
When you are deciding on an activity for your teen put it to the Biblical test.

Romans 12:9
Love must be sincere. Hate what is evil; cling to what is good.

Ephesians 5:11
Have nothing to do with the fruitless deeds of darkness, but rather expose them.

Philippians 4:8
Finally, brothers, whatever is true, whatever is noble, whatever is right, whatever is pure, whatever is lovely, whatever is admirable—if anything is excellent or praise-worthy—think about such things.

Colossians 3:5-6
Put to death, therefore, whatever belongs to your earthly nature: sexual immorality, impurity, lust, evil desires and greed, which is idolatry. Because of these, the wrath of God is coming.

I Thessalonians 5:21-22
Test everything. Hold on to the good. Avoid every kind of evil.

II Timothy 2:22
Flee the evil desires of youth, and pursue righteousness, faith, love and peace, along with those who call on the Lord out of a pure heart.

James 1:21
Therefore, get rid of all moral filth and the evil that is so prevalent, and humbly accept the word planted in you, which can save you.

Romans 16:19

I want you to be wise about what is good, and innocent about what is evil.

Ephesians 5:3-7

But among you there must not be even a hint of sexual immorality, or of any kind of impurity, or of greed, because these are improper for God's holy people. Nor should there be obscenity, foolish talk or coarse joking, which are out of place, but rather thanksgiving.

For of this you can be sure: No immoral, impure or greedy person—such a man is an idolater—has any inheritance in the kingdom of Christ and of God. Let no one deceive you with empty words, for because of such things God's wrath comes on those who are Disobedient. Therefore do not be partners with them.

I Peter 2:21

To this you were called, because Christ suffered for you, leaving you an example, that you should FOLLOW IN HIS STEPS.

CONTRIBUTORS

We would like to thank the parent's and teen's who gave so freely of their time and experiences to contribute to "From the Heart of a Parent." Because of your contributions many parents and teens will be helped. May God richly bless you all.

Connie Millergren
Buddy & Stephanie Bell
Mark & Julie Courson
David & Susan Clark
Doug & Janet Morrison
Howard & Donna Todd
Bill & Peggy Butler
Terry & Cindy Williams
Joe & Debbie Newman
Kellie Segrest
Bill & Janice Pemberton
Wendell & Billie Scroggins
John & Pat Tew
Al & Candie Crosby
Rodney & Mary Jo Shephard
Mark & Jacque Loudermilk
James & Becky Bagwell
Carl Hopson
Ken & Linda Dunham
Joe & Jane Keller
Butch & Roanne Norris
James & Sue Crabtree
Dick & Dorris Thompson
Johnny Hobbie
Paul & Saundra Bozeman
Toni Fowler
Jessica Guy
Billy & Linda Segrest
Pat & Laurie Gregory
Donnie & Nonnie Owen
Jerome & Terry Dees

Louis & Nita Hartzog
David & Martha Jackson
Donnie & Sherrie Hilliard
Ken & Jan Kilpatrick
Milton & Carol Strickland
Barbara Bice
John & Mona Lazenby
Craig & Melinda Hopson
Johnny & Christy Johnson
Danny & Sandy Luster
Michael Johnston
John A. & Allyson Andrews
Rebecca McCartha
Wes Gunn
Roger & Annette Wright
Randy & Donna Stroup
Rocco & Betty Arnold
Don & Linda Torode
Rodney & Deborah Tidwell
Johnny & Lindy Blanchard
Dudley & Vicki Chancey
Bill & Joe Ann Norris
Mitch & Rhonda Temple
Joe & Jackie Miller
Dwayne & Diane Davis
Joy Millergren Smith
Alex & Cindy Jackson
Heidi Brooks
Pat & Deb Watkins
Tommy & Jannett Weldon

Special Thanks to Editors: James Crabtree and Jim Earnhart

Teen Life Ministries Contact Information

Please send us a note about the way this book has influenced your parenting and your family. We would love to hear from you.

Teen Life Ministries
236 Foxdale Rd.
Montgomery, AL 36109
334-277-7726

Check Out:

www.TeenLifeMinistries.com

For more resources to support your parenting.